THE MIRACLE JOURNEY

*Guideposts to Restoration
after Heartbreak and Loss*

Paul Stutzman

All Scripture quotations, unless otherwise indicated, are taken from the Holy Bible, New International Version®, NIV ®. Copyright© 1973, 1978, 1984, 2011 by Biblica, Inc.™ Used by permission of Zondervan. All rights reserved worldwide.

Scripture quotations marked (NLT) are taken from the Holy Bible, New Living Translation, copyright ©1996, 2004, 2015 by Tyndale House Foundation. Used by permission of Tyndale House Publishers, Carol Stream, Illinois 60188. All rights reserved.

Scripture quotes marked (AP) are the author's paraphrase.

Poems by Susan Kocak used by Permission

Copyright © 2021 Wandering Home Books
All rights reserved. No part of this publication may be reproduced, stored in a retrieval system or transmitted, in any form, or by any means, electronic, mechanical, photocopying, recording, or otherwise, without the prior permission of the publisher.

ISBN 13: 978-0-9998874-9-3

TABLE OF CONTENTS

MAKE YOUR CHOICES
- Can These Live Again? 3
- The Unfinished Journey 8
- Dead Bodies and Sledgehammers 13
- Meet Jeremiah 18
- Look for Guideposts 22
- No Shorter Routes 26
- "Return to Me" 33
- Choices and Goals 37
- However-ing 40

DON'T LOOK BACK!
- Don't Look Back! 47
- Restoration is Not Behind You 53
- I Know You Will 59
- "Everything We Wanted" 61
- *Please*, Answers 66
- Chasing a Myth? 71

HOPE IS AHEAD
- Don't Miss It! 77
- After Death, Resurrection 81
- Miracle Mansion 86

Cloud and Fire 91
The Master Workman 97
A Chrysalis Time.. 101
Where's My Hope?... 107
My Only Hope 111

WEEP, WAIL, HOWL
The Breakdown Lane 119
Collecting the Tears 123
The Black Pit.. 127
Breaking, Boiling, Squeezing 132
Crushed, Satisfied 137
This Kindness 143

YOU NEED FORGIVENESS
Forgiveness for the Wounded.. 153
The Only Way 156
Coconut Cake 161
Times of Refreshing 167
Daily, in Bits 172

DINE DIVINELY
The Right Diet.. 179
Life Essential... 183
Cabbage Manna 187
Angel Food and Trail Magic 190

UNWRAP THE GRAVECLOTHES
- Out of Your Graves 199
- Ezekiels 204
- Are You? Will You? 210
- If You Can Use Any of This 214
- Good Proclamations 221

HIS ARM IS NOT TOO SHORT
- How Long is God's Arm? 229
- Bones Can Get to the Promised Land 235
- A New Thing 239

GO TAKE THE LAND!
- The Story in the Scars 247
- Heavenly Garment Shopping 252
- The Message and the Messengers 258
- The End is the Beginning 267

After Words 273

MAKE YOUR CHOICES

Can These Live Again?

A mighty battle filled the air with cries of pain and agony. Spears thrust deep into soldiers and swords left gaping wounds. Shattered and bleeding bodies slumped to the dry, sandy soil, and slowly life and sounds ebbed away.

We aren't told who won and who was defeated. We only know that many lives had been lost. The valley grew silent, a scene of grim devastation. There they lay, an army decaying in the desert until nothing remained but bones. Bones picked clean by nature's scavengers. Bones scattered across the vast valley. Dry, lifeless bones.

God and Ezekiel walked back and forth across that valley, carefully avoiding stepping on bones. This detail is not mentioned in the Bible, but one can surely imagine they would be respectful of the bones. If it were me, I'd be very careful!

God turned to Ezekiel and asked a question.

Before I get to the question, let me clear up something. Some of you Bible scholars already are shouting, "But no one has ever seen God!" I'm one step ahead of you.

God led Ezekiel out to that valley "by the Spirit of the LORD." It's akin to what's often happened to me and hopefully you. The Holy Spirit compels us or prompts us to do something. That's the same as being led by the Spirit of the Lord.

We now return to God's question.

"Can these bones live?" That's what God asked of Ezekiel.

Of course not! That would be the logical answer, wouldn't it? And I imagine it's what Ezekiel thought.

Those bones represented the nation of Judah, their hopes and their dreams. "Our bones are dried up," they said, "and all our hope is gone."

Babylon, the military powerhouse of the day, had invaded Judah. The Temple, center of the people's worship, had been destroyed. The brightest and best of their people—all the intellectuals, the young and strong, the scientists, teachers, doctors, agriculturalists, leaders—had been marched off as prisoners of war to Babylon. Those left behind lived in extreme poverty and fear of their lives. Just going out and looking for food was risky. All the glorious promises God had made to His people seemed to be wiped out; their hopes and dreams were gone forever. Restoration of their nation seemed impossible. Their lives had been destroyed.

Oh yes, my fellow sojourner, we can relate, can't we? Our bones, our spirits, our hopes and dreams have been destroyed by loss. Our self-worth is as dry as those bones. Our life feels as barren as that desert.

Are you feeling totally hopeless? In pain caused by an event that crashed upon you and sent you into a downward spiral? Have you been ripped apart by the spear of a friend's betrayal? Has a lie spoken about you plunged into your life and destroyed it? Has death invaded your soul? Has part of your identity been stripped away, perhaps an ability or a capability or a job, perhaps the one thing you valued most about yourself? Are you mourning the life you once knew, now destroyed by the pandemic, political fighting, and hostile social circumstances?

Are you feeling rejected? Worthless? Has your ability to trust been broken beyond repair? Are you in need of renewed hope after a job loss, the death of a loved one, a relationship gone bad, marriage vows broken, or being a victim of someone else's cruelty?

Perhaps you're actually one who is responsible for many of these dry bones. Maybe you have been the betrayer, the unfaithful, the one who has devastated many lives. Maybe you are the rebellious son or daughter, the one who has shattered trust, the hand that bore a sword plunged deep into another's heart. The truth is that as you destroyed another, you were also destroying yourself. Your bones lie among the others.

Maybe you're one who is frustrated and disappointed with God. Your trust in Him has been shaken and has dwindled to almost nothing. You're angry with Him. How could He have allowed this thing to happen? Or maybe, as the perpetrator of pain, you are now afraid that God will not forgive what you've done. How could He possibly? The bones of your faith are parched.

Whatever the specifics of your situation, are you feeling the naked, deadly hopelessness of bones bleached in the hot sun, stripped of all flesh and breath and life, knowing that not even a glimmer of hope exists?

Are you tired of feeling that way?

There is an invitation awaiting you. It's from me.

I've been invited to go on a journey to a place of restoration. You are welcome to come with me. As a matter of fact, I'm really hoping you will accompany me. Folks are waiting for us along our journey toward restoration. These folks will help us along the way. They have been positioned at just the right place and time to meet our specific needs.

WARNING: This journey is fraught with pitfalls. There will be pain and tears. It is a journey for only the brave and courageous.

Is the journey worth it? Can a person really be made whole again when they are dead on the inside? Can your destroyed spirit, your devastated broken heart be made whole again? Can shattered joy and hope really be restored to you? Is peace possible?

Yes, this can all happen. We will need a miracle, though. And the journey will require a choice and an effort from you. We'll get to those a little farther along in the journey, but be forewarned that the journey is not an easy one.

You can choose to stay where you are and become an island to yourself, isolated and steeped in your own toxic thoughts and feelings. You can attempt to keep the pain at bay, try to dull it, gloss over it, pretend it doesn't hurt. You might think you've kicked the grief monster down the road a bit, but when you meet yourself face to face, you know you are still dead inside. You can remain a miserable person, or....

You can join me on the miracle journey.

The Unfinished Journey

The story behind this journey we are undertaking together began one winter evening when I received an email from a woman who had recently lost her husband. He had died suddenly, but he had wanted to write a book about not waiting too long to do the important things in life. He'd been inspired by reading my first book, *Hiking Through*. His wife wanted very much to see the book he had only dreamed of actually be written. She wasn't sure she could do it alone and wondered if I could help.

We had long telephone discussions and finally decided to meet. We fell in love, a wonderful, beautiful love that I called a "spiritual romance." We both believed this gift of love was a gift from God. For two years, we delighted in the gift. We did so many wonderful things together and made so many beautiful memories—but her husband's book was never written.

Then, suddenly, the relationship ended. For me, it was a brutal, devastating ending. My trust in her was shattered. Any dreams we both had of the future were demolished. I felt deceived. And I soon descended into a pit of feeling rejected, worthless, unwanted, and very much alone.

From the depths of that pit, I spent a summer and part of the fall crying out to God. In the mornings, I'd take my Bible and books out to the glider on my back porch—the old, rusty glider that had once held a place on Mom and Dad's porch—and I would spend time reading and talking with God. I walked and ran on our local rails-to-trails path, and I felt a strong sense of God's presence, clarity of His Spirit's leading, and comfort from the Scriptures as I tried to work through my grieving.

Out of that brokenness and seeking God came a book, *Don't Wait Too Long*. It may be the book the deceased husband wanted to write; I do not know that for certain. I only know how that message applied to my own life and the circumstances I was in, and that's how I wrote it.

If you read *DWTL*, you may have noticed that I did not reach the point of forgiveness. I wanted to forgive the lady. I thought I was "working on it." But as I ended the book, I wasn't quite there.

Finally, in the fall, I determined that I was ready to completely, finally, ultimately, wholeheartedly forgive. I sent her a letter to tell her I'd forgiven her (even though she had never asked for my forgiveness) because I knew I needed to forgive.

And I thought, that was that.

Then came the winter, and I wandered off into the wilderness—although I didn't realize where I was headed.

No more mornings in the sun sitting on Mom and Dad's rusty old glider reading the Scriptures, asking for healing. No more walks on the trail, looking for the Spirit's guidance.

I was off, going down some blue-blazed trails.

Now, blue-blazed trails aren't necessarily *wrong* trails. They aren't necessarily evil. They might even lead to joy and beautiful vistas. But if you are headed to Katahdin, you think twice before you follow the blue blazes.

Before I confuse you further, allow me to explain. If you hike the Appalachian Trail, you begin in Georgia and your destination is a mountaintop in Maine. The official AT is marked with white stripes painted on trees, rocks, railroad ties, and various other markers. You'll follow those white blazes through 14 states, over 300 mountains, through forests and bogs and valleys and farms and towns. You'll walk nearly 2,200 miles—some refer to it as "5 million steps." The journey will take months; and on many days, the challenge will look impossible. But as long as you get up every morning and keep taking steps following the white blazes, you will eventually get to the goal: a sign on the top of the great mountain in Maine called Katahdin.

Along the way, you'll see other trails that are marked with a blue blaze. They lead away from the official AT. They might lead to wonderful views and interesting things to see and do, and they often offer an easier terrain. Sometimes, they do join up with the official AT later in your journey.

But blue blazes will sidetrack you. They'll delay your arrival at the goal. If you want to be a purist and hike the official AT, you'll follow the white blazes to your destination.

In January, I went to Florida, thinking I'd spend my days writing this sequel to *Don't Wait Too Long*. (By the way, this book you're now holding turned out to be vastly different than what I *thought* I was going to write.) But once I had landed in Florida's sunshine, my days were consumed with book signings and meeting people. Then a friend bought a house. It was a wonderful house in a good location—but nothing had been done to maintain it for the last twenty years. My cousin Marv and I were going to do the renovation work so the house could be put back on the market.

During my Florida sojourn, it turned out, I took my eyes off the white blazes and went down a blue-blazed trail. During the previous summer and fall, I had been on the path to healing; but the months in Florida, although pleasant and productive in many ways, set me back in my journey to restoration.

We spent two months doing the work on the house. We worked hard at tearing out, patching, replacing, recreating—but as I worked, I was still wondering, still hurting, still trying to figure out why the relationship had gone awry. Every day, my thoughts swirled round and round, dwelling in the land of broken trust and rejection. I needed restoration as much as the house needed it.

And I realized I was far from the end of the journey that I had begun the previous summer. I wasn't anywhere near truly forgiving my former love. The busyness of my days in Florida sent me off on trails other than the one that led to restoration of joy, peace, and being able to enjoy life. I was consumed by pain and sadness.

I was, as I had read in the book of Jeremiah during my morning times on the glider, deep in the muck at the bottom of a pit. You can read the story in Jeremiah chapter 38. It took 31 men to get him out of that pit. I was trapped in mud just as deep and sticky. And I saw no way out. Escape from the constant pain, questions, and turmoil seemed impossible—as impossible as walking 5 million steps over mountains and through deep valleys.

When the house renovation was finished, I came home—but home only felt barren, hopeless, and joyless.

One spring morning, I heard this clear directive from God: "Move, Paul. Step into your future. Step into it!"

I knew that's what I had to do. I *had* to. I *wanted* to. But I could not. Wandering in a wilderness of grief and desolation, I found no escape.

Have you ever felt you were stuck in a pit or wandering homeless in a wilderness? Have your hopes and dreams been shattered? Have you been wounded and rejected? Have you felt worthless and oh, so lonely? Have you been hopeless and helpless? Maybe you're there right now. Then you understand where I was.

Restoration after devastation—that's what I longed for, but it seemed I had no power to find it or achieve it. My journey to restoration was far from over.

Dead Bodies and Sledgehammers

When devastation hits, some people seem able to just move on. I can't. That's just not my nature. There is so much more to the process of healing for me. I wanted to; I was so tired of the pain. This business of restoration was taking too long! I wanted to be done with it. But when God said "Move, and step into your future," I couldn't because I felt like I was dragging along a dead body.

The apostle Paul talked about being a miserable man: "Who will free me from this body of death?" He was talking about his constant struggle with the flesh, his old desires that constantly fought against everything the Holy Spirit was doing in him.

I realize I've taken Paul's question a bit out of context, but I felt something of that struggle—wanting to move forward as God commanded but held back by a heaviness that felt like a dead, decaying, stinking body that was slowly losing body parts but was still attached to me. I wanted to get rid of it, but it was so hard to do.

We carry bags of bitterness, loneliness, anger, frustration, grief, guilt—you can name what's in your bag. It's hard to let go, even though those things are weighing us down and robbing us of the life of the present moment. Sometimes when we let go of that bag or that dead body, the space that is left fills with loneliness, sadness, and depression. Because, after all, we've become accustomed to whatever that stinking thing is that we're still carrying. It's almost a part of us.

Even when we're dragging something with us that is harmful to us, we are strangely resistant to change. Sometimes I asked myself, *Do you want to change? Do you really want to?* And sometimes, I've thought that I just don't have it in me.

I gave my heart to a lady, and it came back to me in tiny pieces. For over a year, I tried to separate from the pain, the anger, the questions. But they just kept hanging on to me. Especially those thoughts that I'm not good enough, I'm a loser, I'm not worthy. Those lies that Satan whispers stuck with me. They're so hard to get rid of.

I wanted to be restored—back to joy, to love, to hope, to dreams.

This book is not only about my wounds from a romantic breakup. This is about universal wounds and longing for joy and peace and healing. Your pain may be from a death, a divorce, a rejection. You may have lost a cherished pet or been betrayed by a friend. You might be carrying the heartache of a rebellious child or the loss of a child. Perhaps you think you will never heal after your loved one has ended their own life.

Or you are living in the nightmare of emotional and mental abuse. Or your life was turned upside down when you were suddenly stripped of your job. Maybe your faith is starving in the wilderness. And all of us—I doubt any of my readers have been unaffected—all of us are trying to deal with the world coming apart at the seams right now. A pandemic, wildfires, protests, looting, deadly violence, political poison, division, hurricanes, and economic uncertainty invaded our lives in 2020.

I was obviously a mess when I came home from sunny Florida to a world turned upside down and an internal world that was in pain and turmoil. As one of our preachers used to say when I was a kid, I was "so low I had to reach up to touch the bottom." And there was no hiding my sad state of mind and heart. But maybe you're more like a beautiful, giant watermelon I grew one year.

In my childhood, our family had a huge garden. Each of us siblings had a little patch of our own in the garden, a little square where we could plant whatever we wanted. I always planted watermelon. I loved watching a little watermelon seed grow into a plant that produced big melons. Once in a while, I'd get the small round watermelons; I wasn't impressed with those. I loved growing BIG. If I had a good-sized melon growing, oh my, I'd pamper it, weed around it, and water it with great attention and tenderness.

One year, an exceptionally big melon was my prize. I couldn't wait to open it up and eat it. Finally, the day came when it was deemed ripe and ready to give up its deliciousness. I carried it inside carefully. It was a perfect specimen. In the kitchen, we sliced it open.

Let me tell you, there's nothing more disappointing than a watermelon that looks perfect but isn't good. The perfect exterior had fooled me into thinking the inside was good, too, but that watermelon needed a lot of restoration. There's probably a lot of bad watermelons walking around in the world, looking pretty good on the outside, feeling pretty awful inside. On the outside, I was in the best shape I've been in my life. I was running on the trail, my diet was good, I had lost weight, I had that healthy tan… Hey, looks good! On the outside. Inside, there was great turmoil. Are you walking around like this, too?

Or, we might compare ourselves to that house Marv and I renovated. The exterior looked fine. It was in a beautiful location. But the interior was in great need of work. Driving by on the street, you'd have no idea of what the inside looked like.

No matter the specifics of what led to the pain we're carrying and no matter whether we're openly a mess or we're a house nicely painted but needing restoration, we all experience similar feelings after our lives have been shattered. Right now, our lives are like a wandering in the wilderness, an exile, a death even though we go on breathing and hurting, a slow rotting away on the inside.

We need Jesus more than ever. He defeated death on the cross. I had gone to His cross with that dead body hanging on me; but somehow, I went there and I left there with it still attached to me. I knew Jesus is the answer. I knew, as David wrote in the psalms, that God is our only hope. But… *how?* How do we get from where we are now to where we want to be?

How do we escape the pit so that we can even see hope? How do we get rid of the death that has invaded and enveloped us and drags along with us in every moment of every day and night? Whatever it is—your past, your anger, your guilt, your grief, your pain, your loss. And can you get rid of it? Or do you just have to accept it? How do you make peace with it?

As Marv and I were restoring that house, we took out a wall. And to get that wall down, we had to use some brute force. It did not come out gently. It fought us. We took sledgehammers to it. We took saws to it. That wall fought us right up to the time we delivered it in pieces to the dump.

Like that house, we need restoration. There may be walls that need to come down. There may be something that needs to be sledgehammered into pieces and taken away to the dump. The darkness will fight us. I know you know what I mean.

I also know that my own restoration required much more than a little patch and a slap of paint on a corner of drywall.

Meet Jeremiah

On this long journey through my grief, I've met people in the Scriptures and in my life today who knew exactly what I was going through. In *DWTL*, I wrote about King David, whose psalms contain all the tumult of emotions that besieged me. The second person who became important to me was Jeremiah. Yes, the prophet in the Old Testament.

What could Jeremiah possibly know about me? He knew despair, loss, devastation, bitterness, the deep darkness that seems to snuff out hope—every word that I've used in my lamentations over the past year was known and experienced deeply by Jeremiah.

His situation was a bit different than mine. And probably different than yours. He lived during the time Babylon invaded Judah and took Jeremiah's people off to exile in a faraway land. His was a different time and different place, but we can identify with so much of what he went through. He's known as "the weeping prophet" and is believed to be the author of the book of Lamentations. That's exactly what the book is—an agonizing, despairing, wailing lament. The deep wounds in us will recognize and respond to much of what Jeremiah wrote. Feel his grief in these phrases he used:

> Arrows shot deep into my heart
> Filled with bitterness, drinking a bitter cup of sorrow
> Chewing on gravel
> > (a description my grief never thought of!)
> Helpless and devastated
> Surrounded with anguish and distress
> Buried in a dark place like those long dead
> Discarded as refuse and garbage
> Rolled in the dust
> My peace stripped away

This one short passage says it all for Jeremiah and me—and maybe for you, too:

> I cry out, "My splendor is gone! Everything I had hoped for from the Lord is lost!" The thought of my suffering and homelessness is bitter beyond words. I will never forget this awful time, as I grieve over my loss." (Lamentations 3:18-20 NLT)

My splendor was gone. Everything I'd hoped for had been ripped away. My grief was bitter and awful. I felt adrift, homeless.

Jeremiah's grief was deepened by the fact that he knew only too well that the destruction of his people was caused by the nation's serious sin. They had made choices that led to these consequences. And maybe you're in the same place—you're painfully aware that what you're going through now, this terrible suffering and grief, is because you've gone down the wrong path. Intentionally. Or maybe you are "bitter beyond words" at the crumbling of our own nation.

Your story and your wounds may be different than mine, but we are undertaking this miracle journey together, and every traveler can benefit from walking a while with Jeremiah, so I'm happy to introduce you.

I met him the first summer after my breakup, as I sat on the glider on the porch in the mornings and prayed and read and cried and pleaded. Jeremiah came along the path, and over the months, he's offered words that have helped me along the way.

One of the first things Jeremiah spoke to me about was road signs and guideposts: "Set up road signs and put up guideposts. Take note of the highway, the road that you take," Jeremiah advised in chapter 31 verse 21.

I've walked those 5 million steps of the Appalachian Trail, and I made it to Katahdin only because I religiously followed the small painted blazes. I've traveled throughout my life, following signs to many destinations. If we want to go from where we are now in the land of devastation and dead bones to a land of life and hope and restoration, well, obviously, we'll need some guidance, some direction. We need road signs.

And we'll need to pay attention to them because up till now, we sure haven't been able to find our way on our own.

Look for Guideposts

"Dad, what's Burma-Shave?" I was old enough to read the signs, but not old enough to know what it was all about.

It was a late summer day, and I was riding beside Dad in the feed mill's truck. We'd first gone to a farm where the farmer was harvesting oats; there, we loaded the truck with his grain. Dad would deliver the grain to a distant town to sell it. I was excited to be going with Dad. It was always an adventure for me, and maybe, just maybe, we'd stop at a little store along the way and Dad would buy a pack of those pink coconut cakes that I loved so much.

Dad explained that Burma-Shave was a company that made shaving products, and those small red and white signs we were seeing as we drove along were the company's way of advertising.

When I think of guideposts, I always think of those Burma-Shave signs. Some of you remember them. They were nothing like today's huge, in-your-face billboards. Each sign had only one or two lines on it. No pictures. And six or seven were necessary to relay the entire message. They were spaced strategically—you had just enough time to read one sign and wonder about the next, and then the next would come into view and give you one or two more lines of a witty verse with a nugget of wisdom for travelers. The last sign would always say "Burma-Shave."

One of Dad's favorites was printed on six signs:
    ANGELS
    WHO GUARD YOU
    WHEN YOU DRIVE
    USUALLY
    RETIRE AT 65
    BURMA-SHAVE

He always chuckled at this one:
    THIS WILL
    NEVER COME
    TO PASS
    A BACKSEAT
    DRIVER
    OUT OF GAS
    BURMA-SHAVE

One that was obviously a sales pitch for their product:
    NOBODY LIKES
    TO SNUGGLE
    OR DINE
    ACCOMPANIED BY
    A PORCUPINE
    BURMA-SHAVE

And two more worth remembering:
> THE ONE WHO
> DRIVES WHEN
> HE'S BEEN DRINKING
> DEPENDS ON YOU
> TO DO HIS THINKING
> BURMA-SHAVE

> DON'T PASS CARS
> ON CURVE OR HILL
> IF THE COPS
> DON'T GET YOU
> MORTICIANS WILL
> BURMA-SHAVE

Fast forward sixty years. Now I'm wandering in a desert, looking for signs someone has put there to show me the way, looking for nuggets of wisdom.

The definition of *restoration* is *being brought back to a former state or condition*. I've suffered a shattering loss. I failed in many ways, and I failed others. Someone failed me. I desire peace, but it seems unattainable. I want to get back to having joy in life.

Maybe your life has been ripped apart by tragedy. Life will never be "normal" again and "picking up the pieces" is impossible because they've been blown to bits. Maybe you've made a bad choice and gone down wrong pathways, and you want to turn around and go back. But you're so far from God that you aren't sure there is a road back.

When I hiked the Appalachian Trail, those white blazes were my guideposts, keeping me on the right trail. I missed the markings a few times and soon found myself going the wrong direction or having no idea where I was. Then it was imperative that I find the white blazes and get back on the right trail.

It's good to have some type of trail markers along the way. Jeremiah's people were spiritually and geographically far from the life they so desperately wanted. He knew they needed guidance to return to a place of hope, the land of restoration. We all need that guidance.

Look for the signs and guideposts as we journey together to restoration, back from brokenness and waywardness to a place by still waters where "He restoreth my soul."

Last summer, the mornings on my glider with God's Word on my lap convinced me that the guideposts we need are right there in the Book. I started pounding the road signs in the ground, writing them in my phone and my journal. Then I'd step back to read them again, and often they were a bit blurry. The Holy Spirit had to clean my glasses and clear my vision; He had to do it again and again and again. (I even wrote a few of my own Burma-Shave-type verses.)

If you, like me, have been hurt in a relationship, come join me on the return trip. If you've wandered so far from God you don't know which way to turn, walk with us. Perhaps you are grieving shattered dreams, a death, or loss of a job, dwelling in a place of intense grieving, or questioning why God would allow such hurts to enter your life; if so, join us in seeking out guideposts back to joy and wholeness.

No Shorter Routes

Five million steps. That's become an epithet for the Appalachian Trail. Can you imagine walking nearly 2,200 miles?

It's only accomplished by taking one step at a time. Hike whatever section is ahead of you that day, give yourself some nourishment and rest, then get up again the next day and hike whatever comes next. One step at a time.

This miracle journey to restoration is something like that trail. In the early spring days of my AT hike, the weather pounded me. Rain, snow, sleet, storms. Then came summer and heat and bugs. I thought I was going to die as I clung to a tree while a tornado raged through. I was exhausted. Always hungry. Always counting the miles. And many mornings, I just wanted to go home, just wanted to be done.

When you're going through pain, you want it to end. Of course we want the misery to be over!

As I begin to write this, I've been grieving the loss of trust in my relationship for fifteen months. Why does it take so long for this wound to heal?

The fact is, the journey is long—much longer than we would like. Loss requires grieving. Whether you've lost a job or lost a loved one or lost a dream, healing is a process. People experience the process differently, but for most of us, the journey will seem far too long. And there will be days we just want to give up. It will be all we can do just to get up in the morning and take a few more steps.

I've also found wisdom in signposts evidenced in the account of the children of Israel escaping slavery in Egypt and trudging through the desert to their Promised Land.

A quick review of the Israelites history. Jacob was the grandson of Abraham. God had promised Abraham descendants as numerous as the stars and a land his family could call their own. Jacob was living in that land as he began his family. With four different women, Jacob had twelve sons. You can imagine there was some sibling rivalry going on there.

The conflict was especially sharp between Joseph and his brothers because Joseph was the favorite son of the favorite wife. He was a bit brash, too, telling his brothers about dreams he had that someday they would all bow down to him.

So when they had the opportunity, far enough away from home, they gave way to their jealousy. Some wanted to kill the young Joseph, but others didn't want to be quite that cruel. They threw him in a pit until it could be decided what should be done with him. And then along came slave traders on their way to Egypt, and the brothers pulled Joseph out and sold him.

Joseph was sold to a government official who was impressed with the young man and gradually gave him more and more responsibility in his household. Then, the man's wife trapped Joseph in a web of lies and he ended up in jail. For years, he was imprisoned. Then, through a series of events, he was released and, again, rose in power in the Egyptian government until finally he was elevated to the highest level of Pharaoh's officials.

Meanwhile, Jacob mourned his son Joseph. The brothers had concocted a story about finding Joseph's bloodied coat and let their father believe the boy was dead. Many years passed. Then a famine hit, and the brothers were forced to go to Egypt to seek food. They'd heard food was still available in Egypt—stores Joseph had been responsible for building up and saving.

There were some tense moments as Joseph realized who had come to him for help and many tears as the family was eventually reconciled (after the tense moments). Then Joseph had his entire family moved to Egypt, where he gave them choice land to settle on.

That's how the descendants of Abraham came to be living in Egypt. They thrived there for generations—hundreds of years—until they became so rich and powerful that the ruling pharaoh became afraid of these aliens living in his land, and—since Joseph was long dead and no longer protecting them—the Egyptians turned on the Israelites, making them slaves.

The Israelites (Hebrews) were living under horrible conditions. If they didn't produce their quota, their hands were chopped off. At one point, the pharaoh ordered all baby boys killed—a form of population control. Out of that terrible time came the story of Moses, the Hebrew baby hidden in the bulrushes of a river, found by Pharaoh's daughter, and raised in the palace.

It was Moses to whom God said, "It's time to get my people out of Egypt. And you're going to be the one to lead them to a wonderful land I have for them." As they left the land they'd been born in, they headed out into the desert, guided by a cloud by day and a column of fire at night.

For the children of Israel, traveling toward a land of promise, the journey was far too long. They did quite a bit of grumbling, complaining, and rebelling. I think I can sympathize—their journey took forty years! I don't intend to be on this restoration journey for that long, and I certainly hope it won't be that long for you, either. But we can learn many things from their experience.

For one thing, don't you wonder why the journey took so long? Granted, Moses had to supervise the move of more than a million people. That in itself had to be a challenge. But there was a much shorter route they could have taken, one that could have been completed in 11 days. Yet God led them along a different route, one that took two years (is my journey going to be two years?) Then, as they drew closer to the borders of the land God had promised them, all sorts of other events came up that prevented them from actually claiming their land. They moved around in the wilderness for another 38 years.

I have no desire to be wandering in circles, sad and depressed, for another 38 years. As a matter of fact, I would have liked to be done with this grieving months ago. My soul has cried out with David, "Oh, that I had wings like a dove! Then I could just fly away from this mess and have peace." That's from Psalm 55 verse 6, my translation. In that psalm, David laments the betrayal of a close friend, someone with whom he had once shared joys and sorrows and even worship. That person has broken promises, deceived, and manipulated. David's anguish, an accurate depiction of all of us who grieve, is evident in his prayer to God: "Please, listen and help me! My thoughts trouble me. I'm distraught, overwhelmed by this." His thoughts were destroying him. If he could just fly away from it all…

But David could not, and neither can we. Some might try. I've sometimes thought my former love took that route—that she just flew away, happy and uncaring. Why was I left with all the pain, all the grieving, all the wandering around in the wilderness trying to sort things out? Why was I the only one suffering?

As I hiked the Appalachian Trail, I at times lost sight of the white blazes, and first thing I knew, I was going in the wrong direction. If we lose sight of our guideposts, we'll be wandering a bit longer in this wilderness desert of pain. If I would have paid more attention to those white blazes, I could have saved the extra steps. And if we pay attention to our guideposts on the miracle journey, we'll save ourselves a few steps and frustration and distress. Don't misunderstand, I'm not saying that these guideposts will give us a shortcut to restoration. The road is still long. But they will keep us going in the right direction.

When I finally found my way back to the official AT after wandering off, the trail always welcomed me back. I was never barred from resuming my hike, never rejected because I'd gone astray one time too many. Finding the next white blaze gave me a feeling of "THIS is where you belong." You may have some setbacks along the way; oh, I'll venture to say you *will* have setbacks along the way. Some days, I feel as though I've taken one step forward but three steps back. I've taken some giant steps backward on occasion. Maybe you'll even get disgusted with this book and throw it in a corner at some point. But come back to the trail. Come back to the miracle journey. You will be welcomed back, and you won't regret it. This is where you belong.

The blue-blazed trails along the way offered routes other than the Appalachian Trail. Some people also "yellow-blazed." That was the term for hitchhiking. Hikers sometimes yellow-blazed so they wouldn't have to hike the hard parts of the trail. Like David wanting to hitch a ride with a dove, they wanted to skip difficult parts of the journey.

There will be days you want to skip. You want to fast forward. Be done with it. Your thoughts will overwhelm you. Days when it's all you can do just to exist. On the AT, there were many days I just wanted to be done. But looking back now, I realize that if I had taken the option of blue blazing or skipping sections, I would have missed so much—encounters, conversations, experiences, the wonders of the natural world, spiritual stretching. I would have missed an encounter with God that brought me to my face on the ground in tears.

We can't skip the hard parts. We can't fly away and escape the pain. (It will fly right along with us, as you probably already know.) As we'll discover, it is in the hard parts that the miracle happens.

"Return to Me"

The book of Psalms is not entirely lament. Some wonderful songs of praise, joy, and comfort are found there. It's just that in my misery, I found myself often returning to the laments because the writer (David, usually) could express exactly how I was feeling. Usually, David also had a word of wisdom and advice.

Psalm 69 is one of those chapters. The guy was in bad shape when he wrote this: "Save me, O God, for the waters have come up to my neck. I sink in the miry depths, where there is no foothold" (verses 1, 2). He's drowning. It does feel at times that we're drowning, doesn't it? We need help! David wrote that he was worn out and hoarse from calling for help.

He admits he's made mistakes, so we don't know how much of this trouble came from his own bad choices. One line says he is hated without cause and reason. Wave after wave of trouble is hitting him, and he needs a lifeline.

He has a little pity party. "I look for sympathy, but there is none. For comforters, but I found none." When we go through loss, devastation, or betrayal, our sadness wants sympathy.

When he's expressed his pain and distress and raged against those who've wronged him, he suddenly sees hope again and a vision of restoration: "I'll praise God and give thanks! He hears the needy; He will save Zion and rebuild the cities of Judah." After 29 verses of lament and anger, he suddenly shifts to praise and hope.

What makes the difference? He shifts his focus to the God who heals and restores. And then he sees hope.

On my glider one morning, poetry came. Poetry seems to sprout in my mind when I'm either in love or in pain.

> I turn to you in my despair;
> I bow my head and breathe a prayer.
> A prayer for hope, a prayer for peace,
> A prayer that all this pain will cease.
> I raise my head and hold it high;
> I hold my hand up to the sky.
> Your outstretched hand I firmly grasp.
> Safely held, Your love will last.

The key to moving into our land of restoration is our relationship with God. We look to so many other people and places for sympathy and comfort, but while we are doing that, God is saying, "Return to Me!"

That was a message He sent through the prophet Malachi. Yes, I hung out quite a bit with the Old Testament prophets. I think the Spirit led me to those people because they bore messages that we need to hear today. They lived in a different time and different situations, but their wanderings and journeys are parallel to ours. And as God said through Malachi, "I am the LORD, and I do not change" (Chapter 3, verse 6). Now, 2,500 years after Malachi delivered this message, God is still sovereign, and He is still the same God He was back then. His words are meant for us, too.

Malachi preached to the people after they had finally moved back from Babylon, settled again in their land, rebuilt Jerusalem and the Temple, and were actually doing quite well—on the surface. But God's message to them was that they had turned away from Him and were, in fact, robbing Him. They worshipped many things other than God. They were cynical about God, asking "What did we gain by obeying Him?" Evil and arrogance were prospering, and "even those who challenge God escape." Sound like any nation you know?

How did they rob God? Specifically, they were not giving the tithes and offerings He had required. The Word is speaking to us today not so much about sacrifices of crops and animals, but the whole concept of giving God what is due Him. The bigger picture is that they have left God; He is no longer *God* to them.

Is that where we are today?

Does the Lord of the Universe who holds everything in His hands have the reverence and worship from us that is due Him?

Do we hold His Word as truth?

Do we acknowledge and live aligned with the One who created us?

I admit that when I fell in love, I gave to this wonderful lady a part of my heart that belongs only to Jesus. I robbed Him.

But there is hope for you and me, even if our relationship with God is not where it should be!

"Test me," was His message through Malachi. "Bring all the tithes into the storehouse and see what happens. Watch me open the windows of Heaven and pour out great blessings on you. Try it! Put me to the test!" (Read it all in Malachi 3.)

What a challenge for us today. I'm not talking about offering plates. I'm talking about giving God everything that He is due. I'm talking about recognizing that He is God, and returning to our relationship with Him as God and we as His people.

After an initial spurt of popularity, Jesus saw many people turn away from Him because they said His teachings were too hard. He asked His disciples at one point, "Are you going to leave, too?" Peter answered, "Where would we go? You're the only one who has the words of life."

Get to know Jesus. Maybe you have never met Him. Maybe your friendship with Him has cooled. Go back to Him. He is the one person you can always trust completely. He will never lie, deceive, or leave you. He can give you genuine peace. He can lead you to life.

Going to Jesus is where you'll find your land of restoration.

You who seek God, may your hearts live!
Psalm 69:32

Choices and Goals

God has given us an amazing gift—the power of choice. We have the choice of whether or not to return to Him and the choice of whether or not to believe His Word. The choice of whether or not we want to heal. The choice of what we want to be.

Faith can die in the desert. Faith in God, loved ones, and people can shrivel up. We can become cynical and say, "Never again." We can blame God and be angry with Him for letting this happen to us, say we want nothing more to do with a God who would let this happen to us. Like the Israelites, we can scoff at faith and say, "I had trust in God, but what good did it do me?"

It's our choice.

At any one of these guideposts along the way, we can say, "I don't want to go down that road. I *will not* go down that road." Although I warn you, ignoring the guides will prolong your aimless wandering on the way to restoration, and maybe you will never get to that land. You might even know a few people like that, folks who are bitter and angry about things that happened decades ago, still breathing and walking around but with hearts as dead and cold as stone, unable to find joy in today, unable to love.

What happens to you and me along the wilderness road depends on our choices.

The first step in changing anything in your life is admitting the issue. Realize *This is who I am and where I am.* Admit the hurt, the devastation. Your pain is real and cannot be numbed. Your anger is real and cannot be ignored.

A choice is required, the vital choice essential to healing. First and foremost, do you want to heal this wound, or do you prefer to wallow in self-pity, sadness, and depression? In the very first chapter, I warned you that you'll need to make some choices along this journey. Decide now: Do you want restoration?

The next step is visualizing your goal. Can you name what you want?

As I hiked the Appalachian Trail, there were many days that the miles ahead looked impossible. I fell several times—sometimes the fall was serious. My body just wanted to give up and quit. But I had a goal. I'd visualize that sign on Katahdin, the goal of every thru-hiker, and I got up and kept on walking (often with plenty of Vitamin I, ibuprofen).

On this miracle journey, I'm often frustrated that it's taking so long. I've fallen on my face often. But I'm visualizing a sign that says THERE IS HOPE. And I have to get up and keep going. If I don't, I'm making the choice not to pursue healing, restoration, and hope.

The long hike of the AT was accomplished one step at a time. Our journey to hope is one step, one choice at a time.

If you've decided to stick it out on this trek, visualize your goal. Can you name what you want?

I want to be able to trust again and to trust completely. I can't live with lies.

I want joy. I had joy. I feel robbed of that. I want my joy restored.

I want to find hope. I know hope is there, but I want it to be personal and alive in me.

Those are the things I long for, my goals on this journey.

A word about choices that bring you suffering. We can choose to do good or to do bad. We all have experienced suffering because of our own bad choices. But remember that folks in our lives have the same power to make choices good or bad. It could be that you are suffering as you read this book because someone else has made a choice, and that choice has resulted in your current loss, pain, or devastation.

Sometimes our pain is self-inflicted. Sometimes it is the result of others' actions. Sometimes an event that seems totally random causes us great loss. And at times, it is simply the cycles and rhythms of life that fracture our lives.

Pain will either destroy you or make you better. Don't let it destroy you. Become a better version of yourself. That's what our journey is about. Make the choice of keeping on, following signposts, eyes on the goal. We will get there.

However-ing

The children of Israel, finally freed from their slavery in Egypt, arrived at the borders of the land God had promised would be theirs. Instead of taking the short route, they'd been led along a circuitous route that took two years. Finally, they stood at the threshold of their new lives; at last, ready to cross the Jordan River, go into Canaan, and settle into a good life God had promised them, a new life in "the most beautiful, the most glorious, the best of all lands" (see Ezekiel 20:6).

But remember, this vast throng of people had never set foot on the soil of Canaan. Their ancestors had left 430 years before, a family of only 70. These millions of people now arriving and intending to claim the land had no idea of what waited for them on the other side of the Jordan River.

So they sent in twelve spies to gather information about the lay of the land. It seemed the practical thing to do.

The spies came back with their good news/bad news report. "Yes, it's a beautiful, fertile land. However, these guys live in fortified cities. They're powerful. We don't have a chance against them. They'll squash us like bugs."

However...

The Lord had brought them through a "great and terrifying wilderness," fed them, protected them, led them to a good land—the best land—He promised to give them as their own.

However...

The sad story is that their fear kept them from going into that good land. They wandered in the wilderness for 38 more years and died there, homeless. Of more than a million people, only two ever set foot in that land of promise—the two scouts who took a stand opposing the other ten and courageously said, "It doesn't matter what we face there, God has promised us and He'll keep His promise. Let's go!"

But the people followed the fear of the majority of the scouts. For all except two, fear kept them from their best life.

Do you know what God thought of their however-ing? Their actions said plainly they did not believe He would take care of them. His response: "None of those who have treated me with contempt will ever see the land!" (Numbers 14:23)

We've been traveling through this wilderness. God has a life waiting for us. What keeps us from believing Him, grabbing His promises, and going forward to the best life He has for us?

Is my constant lamenting keeping me in the wilderness longer than necessary, going in circles and however-ing? Am I right there at the border, just ready to move into whatever

God has for me, but saying, "However, I can't go ahead before I have closure. I've got to have answers to heal my wounds. What I had was so good, and before I can move forward, I've got to know how and why…"

Or are you and I looking at what we know God has promised us, but we are saying, "However, I can't see how that's possible, because, you know, there is this hindrance, or that fact, or this situation…"

Have we said, "I was sure this was from God; however, look at what a disaster came from it. Can I ever trust Him again?"

Or, "I want to live in the land of promise, the land of healing and restoration and joy. I really do. However, this pain, this depression, this loss is so great, I can't see that I'll ever get there."

We might even be thinking, "God's plan of restoration sounds wonderful, and I want that so badly; however, it might all be wishful thinking. After what has happened, I really don't know if I can believe Him anymore."

Are we, too, treating Him with contempt?

We might scale back our however-ing to it's-good-enough.

There were several family tribes in the Israelite throng that settled on a little less than best. The Reuben and Gad families decided that land on the east side of the Jordan was good enough for them, and that's where they stayed. Half of the tribe of Manasseh also chose to remain there. They accepted the good enough instead of going for the greater good that God had planned.

Our promise is in Canaan, dear fellow exile. We've been in a foreign country and we're trying to find our way back to the place God has said we will thrive. It's a long journey for most of us, and we still have quite a ways to go.

There will be some who find a briefly comfortable spot and decide it will be easiest to stay there. We'll be tempted to seek other places of restoration that are "good enough." Maybe it will be a relationship on the rebound. Perhaps we'll find someone whose friendship will keep the pain at bay for brief times, at least. Or we'll throw ourselves into a new hobby or a cause we'll campaign for. Or we put all our energy and hope into our children's lives. Or we'll turn to addictions and even justify it all: "This is the best I can hope for, given my circumstances." (That's letting circumstances decide the boundaries of our lives. Where is God in that statement?)

If you chance upon those places of comfort along the way, don't stay there. Gad and Reuben were so close. But they settled. When you're so close, I can guarantee that the enemy is going to set up some comfortable spots that will entice you to stay. Or he'll throw enough obstacles in your way that you decide, "It's good enough right where I am. It's all I can do."

Are we willing to accept a lesser good rather than trust God to lead us to the greater good?

You might not understand all this now, but you will when you get to that part of the journey. That's when it's time to look around and find the signpost that says DON'T DESPAIR, YOU'RE ALMOST THERE. See it through. Believe His promises. Go across the Jordan River.

Jesus said, "Trust me. Trust God" (see John 14:1).

It's another choice each one of us must make: Will we believe God's promises of restoration are true? Will we go ahead and take the land, with no however-ing? Will we trust Him and where He is taking us?

What's prolonging our time in the wilderness, delaying our healing?

The children of Israel couldn't enter Canaan because they did not believe God's promises that He would take care of them. After everything they had seen Him do, starting with the plagues of Egypt that convinced Pharaoh to free them, to the parting of the Red Sea, to producing food and water for them and leading them with a cloud and pillar of fire, to defeating tribes that attacked them—after all that, they still couldn't believe God would come through on giving them this land.

Before they even left Egypt, God had promised to bring them out of their misery to a good land (Exodus 3:17). But they ended their years in failure and futility (Psalm 78:33). If we don't follow the guideposts on this journey, that could be our lot in life, wandering around, sad and lost.

Our land of promise, friends, is already prepared for us by God. We just need to go claim it. The way won't be easy. We'll be humbled, discouraged, distressed, and in pain, but we'll keep going forward. Then, when we stand on the edge of that new life, each one of us will again need to make a choice.

When this restoration journey finally gets us to the Jordan, it will take trust to get us across the river into Canaan. Will we be however-ing, or will we be packing up our wilderness camp and saying, "Let's go!" ?

GUIDEPOST
↓ ↓ ↓

DON'T LOOK BACK!

/ 10

Don't Look Back!

At the beginning of this book, we left God and Ezekiel surveying the valley of dead bones, with a question hanging in the air: Can these bones live again?

Now we'll move centuries down the road. God stands looking at a field of death. He's not questioning Ezekiel, but Paul. They're not in Israel, but in Berlin, Ohio.

The hand of the Lord was upon me when he took me out on a promontory overlooking a valley. Across this valley lay bits and pieces of broken trust and destroyed dreams. I recognized every fragment and splinter of this devastation.

The impossible had happened. The one I considered my best friend had broken my trust.

My memory saw, in the distance, a loving family barred from me. Happy hours and shared adventures cut short, ended forever. Lying dead on the landscape were dreams and trust and hope. God and I walked back and forth among broken truth and shattered dreams. Ragged fragments of painful, precious memories pushed up their sharp edges and opened new wounds. God listened to the liturgy of mourning that poured from me as I examined each fatal wound and counted all my losses.

Then His question confronted me: "Can these live again? Can these broken pieces of trust be restored? Can joy and hope rise up, resurrected?"

"Oh, Sovereign Lord, only You know that. However, I would imagine that no, they can't. Trust broken is unequivocally broken."

I was as dead as those bones. Stripped of life. As we walked through the broken pieces, I longed for the good days of before, I wanted answers to my questions, and I wanted to escape the death scene. But my eyes were locked on the carnage and my wounds bled as I relived everything.

Already in our journey, we have come to a guidepost that seems impossible to follow: DON'T LOOK BACK.

It's so hard not to look back when we suffer loss. We so badly want life to go back to our version of normal. I know that men, especially, who lose their spouses are in danger of marrying too soon, thinking, *If I just have a wife, the pieces of my life will be put back together again.*

Any loss is a bereavement, even if the something that is gone from your life actually should have been kicked out a long time ago. It could be a harmful habit or something that adversely affected your physical or emotional health. But when anything is taken from us, whether it's ripped away or we purposely cut it away, a part of *us* is gone. And in its place is a hole that aches to be filled.

When what we have lost was so good—or, at the least, seemed so good—the looking back can consume our thoughts and energies and emotions.

I would guess we are all feeling this sense of loss and mourning right now, in the Season of COVID. We long for the lives we had in the past, for many things we then took for granted that are now canceled, postponed, restricted, modified to the point they're unrecognizable, or gone forever. And it wasn't only the pandemic that caused us loss in 2020. Many other factors affected our lives. You can name them. We've all suffered loss this year.

When good things of the past were torn from us because of another person's choice, we linger long, gazing at the memories of what was before. We analyze what we might have done differently. We agonize for days and weeks and months about how we have been wronged. We ask again and again why the other person can't admit the pain they've caused us and ask for forgiveness. Or "How could he have done this to me?" Or "How could I have prevented this?" Or "What if we had tried this…?" We wonder, as David did, if—or when—God will see fit to give our adversary exactly what is due them.

If we've lost a spouse, God might be our target. "Why, God, did you take my wife?" Or in the event of a tragedy, "Why would You let this happen to our family?"

The questions run on and on, but answers never come, do they?

Yet we keep returning to the dead carcass of a failed relationship. We revisit the devastation of broken trust. We pick at the remains of a betrayed relationship. We try to recreate or resurrect. We put actions and motives—even God's—under a microscope.

We look back, yet the story never changes.

The past is lost. It's gone. It is, in a sense, dead. Yet we look back, and we drag the past's dead body along with us into tomorrow.

Following my broken relationship, I looked back, too. How could she abandon me? How could she break my trust? Why won't she give me answers? How can she so easily go on with her life when I've been destroyed?

My heart and mind became paralyzed, soaked in the memories of the past. Have yours, too?

Can we learn anything from a well-known story of someone whose looking back resulted in disaster?

Two men who were angels approached the gateway to Sodom. Sitting at the gate was one of the very few righteous folks in the city, Lot, the nephew of Abram. He must have been stunned by the urgency and import of the strangers' words to him.

"Lot, get out if this city ASAP. Its sins are so great, God is going to destroy it. Do you have family?"

"My wife and two daughters."

"How about sons-in-law?"

"Yes, two men promised to my daughters."

The wickedness of Sodom and Gomorrah was almost unimaginable. Sadly, only four righteous people were found in that city. Perhaps there were six righteous people, if you count the future sons-in-law. We don't know their standing. But when offered an escape route from impending disaster, they declined. The young men thought Lot was joking, and they stayed behind.

Even Lot hesitated at getting out immediately, so when the family dawdled in indecision, the angels grasped their hands and literally pulled the family out of town.

"Hurry to the mountains," the strangers told them. "Don't stop in the plains, and DON'T LOOK BACK!"

At sunrise, burning sulfur rained from the sky, and the two cities were annihilated.

However, Lot's wife just had to see what was taking place in the city behind her. I'm sure she had good memories there. Her future sons-in-law were still there. Her hopes and dreams of grandchildren resided in that town. She had neighbors and friends. She had a home. She had projects and dreams. All she ever knew or had was being destroyed. She just had to look back for a glimpse of what she had lost.

What a fatal error. Her future lay ahead of her. Other hopes and dreams were yet to come. Her daughters could find men in their new town. Grandchildren could be born. Dreams could be followed. Hope could return. There was life ahead. But only if she were obedient.

Could it really hurt to take a quick glance back? She had been warned, but she disobeyed. She looked back.

She was and is now frozen in time.

Whether a random streak of sulfur hit her or if a miracle occurred, it matters little. She became a pillar in that community. A pillar of salt. A crystallized human.

Has your heart, like mine, been crystallized? Do you feel frozen, trapped, unable to go on because you've been looking back?

Will we be stuck here forever?

MEMORIES

Don't look back.
So said the angel to her.
But her memories lay in the city destroyed.
She must look back.
Memories compelled her.
Her hopes and dreams resided there.
Her friends and neighbors had remained behind.
Don't look back!
But we must.
Frozen in time, she views destruction,
Devastation,
Annihilation.
Forever in time viewed through salty tears.
Hers and mine.

11

Restoration is Not Behind You

Does this guidepost that says DON'T LOOK BACK seem hardhearted to you? Are you standing by the sign, wondering if this is truly a good route for you to follow? Are you doubting that you are strong enough to follow its guidance?

I am aware that some of my readers may be grieving a great loss that's quite different than mine—the loss of a spouse or a child; a disease or injury that has incapacitated you; the loss of your home to a natural disaster; the loss of a job into which you have poured all your energy and passion; the loss of a friendship you trusted completely. To say "Don't look back!" might seem hard and uncaring because what you have lost was a precious, wonderful thing.

Yes, this guidepost might apply more fully to my situation, but stick with me. We are all on this journey because we have suffered loss. We might find some universal truths as we travel together. Just ignore whatever you find here that the

Spirit tells you to ignore, and take to heart what He says will be helpful for you. He is our Guide on the journey, after all, and when some words are meant for you, He'll let you know.

There is something about constantly looking back, longing for what is past, what is gone, or what we don't have, that God warns us will be detrimental to us.

In Luke 9, we see an encounter between Jesus and a man eager to follow Him. "But first, Lord, let me go back and say goodbye to my family," said the disciple applicant.

Jesus replied, "Anyone who puts his hand on the plow and looks back is not fit for the kingdom."

What? Wasn't that an unnecessarily harsh response from Jesus?

I think His point was that if you look back while plowing, you're going to lose your sense of direction and plow crooked rows. His warning was that His followers could not be divided in their attention and lose focus.

I am sure I've plowed some horribly crooked rows over the last few months. And it did not help me on the journey to restoration. As a matter of fact, it kept me wandering in the desert even longer than necessary.

When a person comes to Christ, he or she becomes a new person (2 Corinthians 5:17). The old is gone! The new has come! Now, that's the best news ever, isn't it? God is working a complete makeover on us. But don't we still struggle sometimes with looking back at the old? Don't some of those old, comfortable habits still call to us? Don't we even think sometimes that the old life, well, it was so much *easier and better* in some respects?

We're to live as God's new creation. The apostle Paul described in painful detail the constant battle with the old and warned us the conflict will go on until God restores us fully in a new world. But Paul wrote about forgetting what is behind and looking forward to what is ahead, pressing on toward the goal (Philippians 3:13). That sounds like Jesus' view of plowing straight, doesn't it?

A day is coming when there will be no looking back. God's Word tells us not to get too attached to this world. It's not going to last long. Even the good things of this earth will pass away when He creates His new world. The prophecy is from Isaiah 65:17: "See, I will create new heavens and a new earth. The former things will not be remembered, nor will they come to mind." Another translation says we won't even think about the old world anymore. We will not be looking back and will not be longing for *anything* we experience here.

We sometimes make the restoration journey harder than it needs to be by focusing too much on what is now behind us. Again, I am not saying to those of you who have lost precious loved ones that you must put aside your memories of the past and *forget.* We can never do that. I say "we," because I know what it is to grieve such a loss. I know the black hole of emotions, the struggle to get out of bed in the morning, the sense that you have lost your past, present, and future when you lost your loved one. I know you are feeling that your life ended, too, when you buried your wife. *What is there to life after this?* we have asked. I know. I've been there.

But we must have the proper perspective of the past. (We'll get to that in a few chapters.) No matter what loss we're grieving, we can take comfort in knowing that God made our hearts, these hearts that are now broken, and He understands everything that's going on in our hearts right now (see Psalm 33:15). We might not even be able to articulate what's in our hearts, but He knows. And He has plans for us.

I was on the road to healing for a summer and fall, then I went to Florida for the greater part of winter, and I let myself be distracted from the restoration journey. Maybe I did it intentionally. Maybe I distracted myself. Because the journey can be painful. It takes courage to keep going forward.

The progress we could see every day in our renovation of the house was satisfying, but my own restoration did not progress; it regressed. While I worked, I was also looking back, looking back, looking back. My inner world was in shambles as I wallowed in the pain, questions, and increasing anger about the breakup almost a year before. Why did she do this? How could she say one thing, but do something so contradictory? Daily, I walked among those dead bones, reliving everything as my thoughts and emotions hearkened back to the past.

The lady I loved was a gift giver and card sender. One drawer in my house was full of cards and mementoes. She had presented me with gift after gift. When the relationship ended, I sent back to her everything I could—except for one small Christmas gift.

She had given me a memory book with photos from all our adventures together. That book didn't make it back to her when everything else was shipped out. I could not, just could not part with it. Paging through the book, I revisited all our good times. Every page, every photo, held the love we had found and enjoyed. There were a few times I tried to drop it into the trash. I couldn't do that, either. It was full of good memories.

As Marv and I renovated the house in Florida, tearing and cutting things apart, we did not leave the debris lying in the house. We got rid of it. But holding on to that little picture book was like letting a big board lie in the middle of the room and constantly stumbling over it as we tried to renovate and create the new.

Every day, I thought about Her. I wasn't hoping she'd be back. No, I was dwelling on the rejection, the hurt, and the puzzle of *WHY?* The constant battle in my mind was only intensified by that big board lying in the middle of the room; it needed to go, but I left it lying there.

I needed to get rid of that book of memories. The relationship was over. Yet I held onto it for more than a year.

Finally, I knew the trash of demolition had to be taken to the dump. Not literally, in the case of the book. I decided I would send it back.

Apparently, current "breakup wisdom" includes two dictates: 1. Get rid of everything from the old relationship and 2. Have no contact with your ex. I'd done fairly well with the first commandment. Except for that book. But now I was ready to remedy that situation; and as I did so, I deliberately broke the second commandment. I wrote a letter.

The letter was composed one small section at a time. It was so painful. I couldn't do it all at once. But when I finally finished, I felt—in my vast wisdom—that it was "right." I had written openly and honestly. I told Her I was seeking healing.

I wanted to let go of the past and be able to trust and love again. Could she help me by answering a few simple questions?

It felt good to write the letter and send it off with the book. Once I had answers to those questions, I was sure healing would come more quickly.

I was still looking back, thinking the key to answers, healing, peace, and restoration was back there... somewhere. If I could just sort things out.

However, our restoration is not behind us. We are standing at a signpost that says: DON'T LOOK BACK.

But it's so hard not to.

I Know You Will

Back in the days of my restaurant management, we used to tell employees, "Don't bring your problems to work. Leave them at home."

Well, that's a useless statement. If you're going through pain at home, you're going to bring it to work. It's just what happens.

Likewise, we can say DON'T LOOK BACK, but you and I both know you're going to do it.

Remember the story of Enoch, who walked with God? When God invited Enoch to go home with Him, do you suppose Enoch looked back? No, Enoch didn't. He said, "I'm outta here." He might be the only person I know of who never looked back.

We have a tendency to look back; even when it's painful and we've promised ourselves we will *not* go there, we do.

So when you do look back, I'd like to point out a few other signs you might notice behind you. As a matter of fact, you would do well to search for these signs as you're looking back. Take them to heart. They'll be helpful.

Looking back can throw you completely off track. When I hiked the AT, one of the hikers I met lacked a good sense of direction. I called him Garmin. The slightest distraction could confuse him and turn him around. We would meet him going south when we knew he wanted to be going north. We'd turn him around and send him off again in a northerly direction. After all, if you want to get to Katahdin, you've got to keep walking in the right direction.

One of the signs I hope you see as you turn around and look back will be the largest sign. It's the most important one. It says: USE YOUR GPS.

Use **G**od's **P**ositioning **S**ervice. Make this your guide. I hope you'll be referring to it often as you catch yourself looking back. Do everything you can to stay tuned into your GPS. Actually, that's what this book is about—staying tuned into what God wants to do in restoring our lives.

See? I am assuming you will be looking back. I know you will. You will stand at this guidepost that tells you not to, and you will. I did. I still do at times. Why are we compelled to look back? What makes it so difficult to keep our eyes forward?

13

"Everything We Wanted"

During the months I worked hard physically in Florida, my mind was always looking back. It was my habitual stance: peering back over the two years the lovely lady and I had been together and the year since we had been apart. It's doubtful I took two steps forward on the miracle journey during that time. I probably even ran back and lost ground.

But I had lost something so good, so wonderful, that I could only look back at it and grieve.

We are compelled to look back at the past because (we think) it was pretty good.

As the Israelites left Egypt, they moved down the road with a promise. God was rescuing them from their slavery and taking them to a good land that would be their own. They would live there under His blessing and protection as His chosen, special people. He provided for them on their journey, guiding them, providing food and water, preserving their shoes and clothes—their clothes never wore out. (Interesting detail, right?)

But they weren't too far into the journey when they began to complain. They were tired of the manna God gave them as food. They looked back to the rich land they had in Goshen, Egypt, and they started thinking about the meat and fish they had to eat back then. And once the whining and wishing started, it snowballed. Not only meat, but all the trimmings—oh, for some cucumbers, melons, leeks, onions, and garlic. "We had all we wanted back in Egypt!"

Of course, Moses heard all the grumbling. Moses was so fed up with the people that he told the Lord, "If this is the way this is going to go, just kill me now. Spare me from having to deal with these people!"

God heard the grumbling, too. He was angry. After all the care and protection He had given these people, now they're unhappy because they don't have certain foods?

Like the woman turned into a pillar of salt, their looking back also had unhappy results. God sent them meat. Plenty of it. Flocks of quail were blown in, and the people gorged themselves. Those who had been complaining fell sick with a plague, and many died.

I've spent a lot of time looking back toward Egypt, wishing for all the good, the joy, the love I had back there. It was a beautiful love story.

Good memories aren't bad things. Could we even say they are a gift? Surely God had His reasons when He gave us the capacity to remember. But we have this irrational tendency to sort through memories and think only about the cucumbers and melons. As the complainers' mouths watered for fish and leeks, they completely forgot the pain and suffering they had lived under in Egypt. They were slaves! Joseph had died long before, his protection was gone, and a jealous pharaoh stripped away their independence, their wealth, their good life. Now the slavedrivers demanded more and more work. If they didn't meet their quotas, their hands were chopped off. Their babies were killed by the government in an effort to keep their population down.

But all they were thinking about was food.

In my desert, I looked back. I thought about all the wonderful things I shared with a beautiful lady. But I tended to forget that there was also stress in that relationship. It wasn't all idyllic romance. There was some pain and frustration.

When I looked back, I saw the sign that says DANGER: DON'T GLOSS OVER THE TRIALS AND THE PAIN. It was time for me to look back and see the best characteristics in my past love and also the worst ones. She wasn't perfect. Our relationship wasn't perfect. And I wasn't perfect. Besides remembering the wonderful parts, I had to face the things that bothered me, too, not only the small things but the events leading up to the breaking of our relationship.

Are we doing the same thing as the Israelites as we travel through the COVID wilderness? We were living our "normal," everyday lives, taking most of it for granted, assuming many things would always be part of life. Now, we've lost that past "normal." Yes. Our pre-2020 life is gone. Are we whining and complaining to God about what we've lost? But how much of that life was perfect? Were there things that needed to be changed and even stricken from our lives, and now a pandemic has done that?

What does your GPS say?

The bottom line is that in the wilderness, the Israelites wished for something different and somehow quit trusting God and His provision and plan. Their longing for what was behind them wasn't just irrational; the danger in it was that it overrode their trust in their God.

They'd witnessed the Red Sea being blown to dry ground so they could pass, the majesty and holiness of God at Sinai shaking the earth, the cloud and fire that guided them constantly, and the food God sent them every day. But they were getting bored with the manna and they started wishing for something else. They grumbled about what God was giving them. In their looking back and longing for what was behind them, they were actually rejecting God and His plan for them.

The journey can get long and hard and even sometimes boring. If you're looking back, I hope your eyes rest on the sign that says, LOOK BACK FARTHER. Look to the past to see when God was with you. Look at all He's done in your life. He's been there with you through loss of your loved one, or through job changes, or through the loneliest of times. Look back to the day you realized that He loved you so much He died for you. He has parted seas and provided for you, too.

Be grateful for the blessings He's poured into your life, and hold onto your trust in what He is doing now.

I know we've got to leave the past behind. But sometimes the past really was pretty good, and we want that again.

Perhaps death has torn you from your loved one. Not a romantic breakup, but a wrenching from life itself. I know what it is to be down that black hole of grief. I also know that our God is the God of all hope, that He can be trusted, that He is close to the brokenhearted, and that He knows and understands every pain and can give peace.

The Israelites looked back because they didn't trust God with the future. Can we trust God with our future? Can we believe He is always working for our good? This is what faith is—believing something is true, even though we can't see or imagine it.

Whether it was toxic or beautiful, the past is gone—but ask God for a proper perspective on it. And look back as far as you can. God knew you even before you came into this world and began your earthly journey. Has He ever abandoned you? He never will. Don't abandon your faith in Him.

Please, Answers

Sometimes, I think God is so far behind me that I can't figure out what He's trying to do; and at other times, I'm lagging so far behind Him that I can't hear what He tells me to do.

My mind insisted on trying to figure out *why.* Why did this happen? Why won't she answer my questions? Why did God bring us together in the first place? Why? Why? Why?

I had been praying for love. I was ready to be in love again. Then I met Her. And I believed God gave me that gift. It was an incredible love story. We both were sure God had brought us together for a purpose. Her husband had wanted to write a book but had died before he could accomplish that. Were we meant to write the book together? That could be an awesome thing, right?

But we never did anything about the book. In that regard, I failed Her. I got distracted by her beauty, her kindness, the good times we had. I was enamored by her. Did the plan fail because I didn't pursue it? Was there such a plan in God's intention?

And I never had answers from Her. I sent back the memory book and the honest, vulnerable letter humbly asking for answers to my questions. No answers came. Silence.

Why wouldn't you give answers to someone who is hurting and is desperate for those answers? Why not just tell the truth? It seemed that answering my questions should be so easy. Why keep me wandering in this wilderness?

If only I had answers…

Perhaps you've said the same thing. "If I could understand why…" "If only I knew…" "If only he'd tell me…"

You married the perfect man, and now he abuses you. Your teenager ended her life at 15. You devoted your life to a church, and it is now divided by civil war, splintering, and falling apart. You helped your neighbor with his big project, and now you find out he's been spreading rumors about you. You finally retired from that high-pressure job that kept you from your family all these years, and then within weeks, your wife died.

This devastating thing that has torn your life apart—have you been able to figure out *why?*

In most cases, we will never know *why.* I wasn't angry with God, but I was very frustrated that I couldn't find the answers I felt I needed. I think I'm pretty smart (although sometimes I know I'm really stupid), and I thought I should be able to figure this out.

Was I being punished because I had wronged other people? Did our relationship fail because we failed God's plan for us to write a book? Instead of giving me a lasting love, did God have us together to break me, destroy me, so that He could rebuild a better me? And why won't *She* answer my questions? Questions, questions, questions. I like to figure things out. I need answers.

Then, completely unexpected and unimagined, a stranger pointed me back to my GPS.

A reader sent me a quote from my own book. I have never met this person. But she had read *Hiking Through* and felt compelled to write to me about some of the things in that book that had spoken to her. Among other lines, she reminded me of the time I was on the trail and questioning God about why He did not put an end to evils in this world.

> I had boldly (and perhaps foolishly) asked, "God, I have another question. Why do You allow young and innocent children to be harmed? If You are in control, why does that happen?"
>
> His reply was, *Son, if you knew the answer to that, then you would be God.*
>
> So many things in life are a mystery; so many things I cannot possibly understand. I decided to just let God be God, and accept whatever He chose to reveal to me. What I could not comprehend, I did not need to know.

God is God, and I am not. And what does God say? When I throw my *WHY* questions at Him, all I hear is, *I have a plan, and My thoughts and ways are far beyond anything you can imagine.*

Our thinking is so limited; our perspective is so narrow. God's thoughts are so much higher, and they're always about caring for His children. There's that verse that everyone loves to quote from Jeremiah's book, chapter 29 verse 11: "'For I know the plans I have for you,' declares the Lord, 'plans to prosper you and not to harm you, plans to give you a hope and a future.'" Those words were sent as a prophetic message to the exiles in Babylon, whose lives had been devastated and who were living as a subjugated race in a foreign country. Don't you suppose they were looking back? Longing for what they'd lost? Yet God told them, "My plans for you are good."

Oh—there's one other thing. Their current situation would last 70 years. Could you hold onto God's promise that long? I'm sure they had questions. They had been devastated. How could their destroyed nation ever recover? How would they ever be able to return and rebuild? How could they even survive that long in the very pagan country to which they'd been taken?

God is asking us to trust Him, asking us to believe He really is God. His ways are so far above our thinking that we can't comprehend. He promises us that He is always working for our good. Again, this all takes faith, believing in what we cannot possibly see—or figure out on our own.

God *is* God, and I am not. Yet I still grapple with wanting to understand what He is doing. And sometimes, I just wish He'd hurry up with the plan! I don't have 70 more years...

(By the way, God's plan for those people defied all human logic. No one could have imagined what God arranged. He used a pagan king to send the people back to rebuild their city and their lives. The king even funded some of the restoration!)

The questions my letter asked of Her are left unanswered. She followed that rule of No Contact With The Ex. And if she answered truthfully, would it have done more harm than good? Would it have brought pain to her and maybe even her family? (Thinking about some of the things I've done in the past, I'd probably be too embarrassed if I were asked to explain *why*.) Would her answers hurt me even more than I was already hurting? If she told me "the truth," would I even accept it as truth?

Perhaps the words I wrote years ago were meant for me today: "What I cannot comprehend, I do not need to know. I must let God be God."

Is it okay if I never get answers to my questions, even those that drive me crazy? Is it okay with you if there are some things about your situation that you can never figure out?

Will we trust God even though we can't see or understand what He's doing?

Chasing a Myth?

CLOSURE: (1) an act of closing; the condition of being closed (2) an often comforting or satisfying sense of finality. (Merriam-Webster)

I found myself wondering, "If I've forgiven Her, why do I still care about answers?"

"Well, it's about getting closure," I told myself. "If I don't get that closure, can I ever move into restoration?"

The "right" answer is, obviously, Yes, you can.

But how do you do it?

One of the reasons we keep looking back and keep asking questions that get no answers is because we are looking for closure. I thought I had to have closure so that the open wound could heal. The guideposts along the way to restoration were looking a bit blurry to me. How do I move on without closure?

Here's another question: When we chase closure, are we chasing a myth?

Neither of Merriam-Webster's two definitions of closure given above seem applicable to our miracle journey.

The devastation we've gone through is not like a book where, when you've finished reading, you close it, put it away, and are done with it. Wait. Maybe that's not a good example. Really good books that have an impact on you are never "done" with you. They have left their mark. You've changed because you read their words. Even weeks and months after you closed the book and put it on the shelf, the words or ideas from that book are a part of you.

These losses we've experienced are like that. They have left their mark—scars, in most cases. They've changed us, in good ways and bad. The valleys we've walked through will have influence on us for the remainder of our lives. Any suffering, loss, or heartbreak you bear will leave its mark and change you in some way. It is never "closed."

Really, the only book that is put back on the shelf and truly "closed," finished, done, is one that has had no impact on you. It put you to sleep. It was quite forgettable. Nothing in those pages touched you in any way. Maybe you couldn't even finish reading the book. Maybe you didn't put it back on the shelf but instead threw it in the trash. Few things in our lives—good and bad—are truly like that, closed and final and without any lasting effect.

At one time, I reasoned that if I only had answers to my questions, I would find closure and be able to heal and move on. Then I realized that even if I was given answers, they might not make sense or satisfy. That reality defies definition

#2 above. Answers from Her probably wouldn't have given me comfort, satisfaction, or finality.

And, let's face it, the person who has dealt you devastating blows is not the person who is going to help you heal. If they've lied to you, why would you expect them to tell you the truth? If they've betrayed your trust, why would you think they'll be concerned about your well-being? If they've divorced you, why would you look to them for healing of the wounds they inflicted? If they've died without giving you their forgiveness or an apology or reconciliation, well, then, you will never have that closure you say you need.

If you must look back and dissect and analyze, look back to see what part you have played. What has God shown you must change in your life? Where do *you* need to ask forgiveness? What has He taught you? Whatever event has battered and almost destroyed you is not closed and final. It has left its mark on you. I know God is changing me on this journey. I even feel that He's preparing me—for what, I have yet to discover.

Perhaps we cause our misery to continue longer than necessary by refusing to accept reality. Our love was dead. But I kept kicking at it, trying to restore it. I was convinced that we could still communicate heart-to-heart as we once did. If She only cared enough to answer my questions…

But it was over. I was still looking back, looking back at a dead thing. However, my quest for answers never stopped. I thought I needed closure.

In almost every aspect of life, we have no such thing as closure. People leave their footprints in our lives—and some leave scars. Events good and bad shape us; or, rather, we are shaped by our response to events. Few things in our lives are "final." And many, many things can leave us hanging with no sense of satisfaction or comfort.

The questions and my quest drove me to the edge of sanity. Is it too harsh to say that grief is a form of mental illness? If there is no such thing as closure, how do we go on?

Isn't it peace that we are really seeking?

Jesus offers us peace, and He said He gives it to us "not as the world giveth." Is "closure" the world's unsatisfactory imitation of Jesus' peace? Yet the world can't even give us that.

Jesus' peace "surpasses all understanding." We can't explain it or define it. It's one of the miracles of the miracle journey: His peace guards our hearts and minds (Philippians 4:7). Jesus tacked this onto His promise about giving us His peace: "So don't let your hearts be troubled" (John 14:27). A heart that can remain untroubled, no matter what comes my way, is what I want.

If you check your GPS, you'll see it ignores the mythical closure and points you straight to Jesus and His peace.

GUIDEPOST
↓ ↓ ↓

HOPE IS AHEAD

16

Don't Miss It!

Enough looking back.

It may be obvious, but allow me to point out that when we're looking back, we're going to miss whatever's ahead of us.

It's time to turn around and look ahead. Let's catch a glimpse of what we can look forward to. You might find it difficult to believe any of this right now, but it will come. It's up ahead. And that's where we're going.

The past is behind you; there's no way to relive it. This stretch of the road is not your home, either. You aren't staying here. Your life was uprooted somewhere in the past, back there behind you in the journey. Don't let your roots go down here in the wilderness. God is doing something up ahead, and that's where we want to be.

Someday, you will be the one standing by this highway sign and reassuring other travelers that this guidepost is truth.

I haven't checked, but it's possible that in every book I've written, two things have always popped up: the Valley of Baca and monarch butterflies. Get ready... they'll be in this book, too.

A passage from Psalm 84 is well known in my family because my Uncle Roman loved to quote and expound on these three verses. They speak of those who have set their hearts on pilgrimage and draw their strength from God. Those pilgrims are blessed, and as they pass through the Valley of Baca, they make it a place of springs and pools. They go from strength to strength on their pilgrimage, until finally they come to their destination—the presence of God in Zion.

The Valley of Baca is also translated as the Valley of Weeping or a "dry valley." That might be where you're traveling right now. In my mind, I can see this signpost along the rough road that winds through the Valley of Weeping: HOPE IS AHEAD. Hope is what can turn the dry valley into a place of refreshing pools. Hope is what propels us on from one strength to the next.

And someday, yes, it might very well be you standing next to this signpost in the Valley of Weeping and assuring all battered, weary travelers that, indeed, it's true—hope is ahead.

We aren't going backward on this journey. I know, we may waver or stumble or get disoriented and take a few steps back every now and then; but our future, the rest of our lives, is up ahead.

Right now, though, we may feel like a pillar of salt standing outside the smoldering ruins of Sodom. If our hearts likewise have hardened and we cannot move forward, then we need another miracle.

Our friend Ezekiel comes along beside us to tell us there is hope. Just a few chapters before his visit to the valley of dead bones, Ezekiel was given this message from God to deliver to the children of Israel—and now, to us.

> "I will sprinkle clean water on you, and you will be clean; I will cleanse you from all your impurities and from all your idols. I will give you a new heart and put a new spirit in you; I will remove from you your heart of stone and give you a heart of flesh." (Ezekiel 36:25-26)

In the Bible, water is often the symbol of a cleansing, life-giving and life-sustaining element. Rain and streams are renewal and refreshment. Two verses in Job 14 speak about a tree cut down, its stump dying, "yet at the scent of water it will bud and put forth shoots like a plant." I read that and longed for a scent of water that would bring life back to me or the sprinkle of clean water that would give me a new heart. My old heart was in pieces. Dead.

Ezekiel's message is that God can do something new. A new heart? I'd call that a miracle.

The thing is, God is all about doing something new in our lives. At one point, He speaks through the prophet Isaiah and says to His people, "Look! I'm doing a new thing! Can't you see it? I'm making a pathway through this wilderness, and creating streams in the desert" (Isaiah 43:19, my paraphrase). The book of Isaiah is filled with such hope of restoration. Chapter 42, verse 9 says (again in my words), "The past has happened; it's done. I'm declaring new things for you." When Jesus entered our history, God announced He was making a new covenant with mankind, giving us a new way to be in relationship with Him. When a person comes to Him, God's Word says the old is gone and He will make us into new people. Colossians 3:10 says our new self is being renewed—in the image of our Creator! In a letter to the Romans, Paul wrote about renewed minds and living in the newness of life. And in the end, God has promised to make new heavens and new earth, an entirely new creation.

God is doing new things. And He doesn't want us to miss it.

I know God's doing new things in me as I travel this path in the wilderness. Sometimes, though, I'd like more insight on those new things. I do know that loss of love and trust destroyed me. I was in a thousand pieces. And my hope says that when God takes those pieces and puts them back together, it will be a new thing.

He asks us to trust Him. Will we?

There is a fountain of ever-flowing, life-giving, spiritual water. He makes streams even in desert places. There is hope for your shattered heart. Your new heart will once again discover the power of love, the potential of hope, the possibilities for dreams to become reality.

They're all in front of you. Up ahead.

17

After Death, Resurrection

As Marv and I tore out the old to make way for the new during our renovation project in Florida, the house fought us. It really did seem at times that the building was a force, throwing up a resistance to our efforts.

I've already said this, but we need to acknowledge and accept this fact: This journey to restoration is hard. We'll get discouraged and want to quit at times. Many times, I've said to myself that I would rather be back on the Appalachian Trail, physically battered and exhausted, than to be here on this healing journey that leaves me emotionally and mentally pummeled and drained. This journey is so much harder.

You will get tired, too. The pain doesn't go away immediately. And every day, you'll have to make the choice: Am I going to take a few more steps forward on this journey?

Those small choices often seem inconsequential. We might carelessly choose, for example, to ignore that signpost that says DON'T LOOK BACK. "Just this once, for this one conversation during coffee break," we reason with ourselves and give ourselves permission to spend the time talking and thinking about how angry we are and how cruel the ex-spouse was. Just this once, we're going to look back and lament. A small choice, it seems, but it will have an effect on the journey.

Every day, we have to make choices that believe there is hope, that there is a future, that everything else we're going to consider in this section is reality.

And if we really want this miracle to change our lives, every day we have to make a decision to die.

At the beginning of my wilderness time, I thought that my restoration would happen if I could only find my way back from the death I'd been dealt. But I've found that restoration comes through my choice to die.

> Then [Jesus] said to them all: "Whoever wants to be my disciple must deny themselves and take up their cross daily and follow me." (Luke 9:23)

My number one priority is still following Jesus. The torment of my mind and heart overshadowed this desire for a while. When you are carrying great pain, it is at times difficult to think about anything else. But following Jesus Christ is still my greatest desire.

In this statement, Jesus is clear that He is giving a life principle for anyone who wants to be His disciple. So that must apply to me, too, and in all circumstances—He says this dying is a "daily" necessity.

What is your cross?

You've heard people say (often with a deep sigh), "This must be my cross to bear." That implies that the cross is a burden, a responsibility, an unescapable fact of their life that they must learn to live with. But that's straying from Jesus' example.

When Jesus picked up His cross, He was going to die on it.

Are we willing to "take up our cross," knowing it means we have to die on it?

How do we die on that cross daily?

The key is there in Jesus' words: "deny themselves." Every day, there's a decision to be made. Am I going to do things God's way or my way? Am I going to be following God's agenda or my agenda? Am I going to pursue God's desires or mine?

If I deny myself, then the answer must always be "God's."

Oh, you and I have a choice and we can make bad choices. God allows it. Our selfishness can say, "I will. I want."

But Jesus has modeled this for His disciples, saying, "Not my will, but thine be done."

Every day and multiple times a day, I've got to crawl up there on the cross and say, "Not my will, but thine be done." The cross isn't pleasant. It's not easy. It's painful to set aside our own desires and plans.

Here is the miracle: Jesus' answer to this daily death is resurrection!

This dying is not to annihilate our personalities, to crucify our wills, or to squash our souls. This dying is so that we can find greater life. He doesn't destroy my will; He resurrects a transformed will. He doesn't snuff out my soul; He resurrects a transformed soul. It's through dying that we find the real life He wants to give us.

In Romans 6 verse 4, we read, "Just as Christ was raised from the dead through the glory of the Father, we too may live a new life."

Another translation says, "We too may walk in newness of life." That's restoration. That's what I want. God says we can have it!

All of this might be too much to think through right now. I did say, just a few paragraphs back, that deep and consuming pain can make it almost impossible to think clearly. So if you need to, put these ideas aside for a while, and come back to them later in our journey.

But I want you to be sure of this: Jesus' answer to death is resurrection and new life is ahead. It comes through a daily, step-by-step, intentional process, getting up every day and taking a few more steps—and dying once again.

About five years ago, a reader of one of my books called me. He and his wife were visiting our area and staying at a local B&B housed in a barn on a farm where my grandfather once lived. I met him there and walked through the building, reminiscing. In the basement that has not been renovated as lodging space, I found the granary where my uncles had long ago scribbled words and names on the walls.

As we were saying our goodbyes, this man reached into his pocket and gave me a little glass bead. It was painted red. "This represents the blood of Christ," he said.

I carried that red bead in my right pocket for years. Every time I reached into the pocket, the bead was there, reminding me of Christ dying for me. Eventually, all the paint wore off, and not a flake of red was left.

After *Don't Wait Too Long* was released, this man emailed me again, telling me he'd read *DWTL*. I related the fate of the red bead. It was now a clear glass bead. I got a note back from him that said, "Clear as Christ's cleansing."

Crucifixion cleanses. And after crucifixion, resurrection!

18

Miracle Mansion

Healing is a battle. After devastation hits, we are in so many pieces that we aren't sure we can find the resources to survive.

Then eventually we come to a place where we know we are going to live, even though all life seems to have drained out of our hearts, minds, and souls.

And we discover we are locked away in a prison.

I wanted to move on in the journey to restoration, but I found myself trapped. I searched for a door to freedom, but the walls of my prison seemed unassailable.

She had dazzled me. That wall was built immediately when I met Her. As I learned to know Her, I fell in love with her inner beauty. That love became another wall, holding me. A third wall grew piece upon piece, built by her kindness and generosity. One more wall was the beautiful trust we shared.

I was almost immediately a captive—but it was a really nice prison, and I was happy.

Two years later, when there was no longer a "we," those walls that held me made it seem impossible for me to let go of the relationship and move into healing. I truly felt imprisoned, and it was no longer nice; it was tortuous.

How to break free?

I thought there must be a door somewhere, a door of truth that would set me free. And I thought She held the key to that door to freedom. If she would just answer those questions I had sent in my letter, the door of truth would appear, she would unlock it, and I would be free. In my mind, that letter had been a letter to my jailor, to the one who had imprisoned me and now would not let me go. I wanted her to use that key—just tell me the truth, please, unlock the door, and let me go on to peace and freedom.

I don't know how you'd describe your prison. Maybe you've lost a spouse and you're sitting behind walls of regrets and thoughts of "what if?" or "if only." Maybe you've lost a job, and you're held immobile by self-recrimination or bitterness or feelings of worthlessness or thoughts of suicide. Maybe COVID has bound you with fear as it uproots everything you used to love about your life—your social life, sports entertainment, even family connections—and you're paralyzed by the disintegration of life as you knew it. Maybe the wrong candidate won on November 3, and you can't get past an immovable wall of despair or anger.

The signpost in this section of the journey says HOPE IS AHEAD. You're probably wondering where the hope is in this scenario of imprisonment.

Well, here's the hope: You have the key to open your prison door.

Sitting dejected in my prison, I thought She had built those walls that held me. I thought She held the key to the door of truth and was withholding it from me. But I was blind. One day, light broke through the gloom in my prison and I realized that I had created the walls myself, and the door is locked on the inside. All the time, I had been holding my own key to my peace and freedom. I was my own jailor!

We can escape our prisons.

And the miracle of the journey is this: We not only open the door, we also break down the walls. We demolish our prison. Then we rebuild, putting pieces back together but tossing out the undesirable parts.

And we build a mansion.

I want to build a mansion in which I can love again, but there are pieces of the old prison that I must eliminate as I rebuild. I was a little possessive in my relationship with Her. Maybe a bit arrogant.

There are pieces I'm eager to use in the rebuild—I've discovered that I have an artesian well of love to give, and I can also be an honorable man. Remember the parts of you that still exist, your passions, the things you enjoy, your talents. The new mansion you build may express those things in a different way than before the devastation, but they are still there for you to incorporate into the mansion you'll build.

Let's look at the devastation caused by the pandemic. There is a miracle journey back from this virus. We can't look back, although we want to. I know we just want to go back to "normal" life, but we can't. Life is ahead of us, not back there.

We're traveling forward, not backward. As we rebuild and glue pieces together, we see that there were things in that "normal" life that weren't good, that we want to do differently as we rebuild our lives into a new normal.

It's probably impossible to believe now, but one day we may say that what has happened to us is both the worst thing that ever happened to us and the best thing that ever happened to us. We've been given a chance to rebuild and to move from a prison to a mansion.

There are so many other metaphors for this. Stained glass is one of my favorites. Stained glass makes use of broken pieces to create a new thing of fascinating beauty. I love stained-glass art. The ancient Japanese art of Kintsugi is the practice of taking broken pieces of pottery and gluing them together with a precious metal like gold or silver. Breaks, cracks, and jagged edges are not hidden, as we so often attempt to do. The rebuilt vase or bowl is prettier than ever because the scars are lined with gold filigree.

The miracle is that new beauty can come from our broken pieces, our hurting wounds, and our life lessons.

And if we put the work into the hands of the Master Creator and allow Him to be the architect, mansions can come from our prisons.

After we had talked about our prisons and mansions, a friend wrote this and sent it to me:

> Looking about me
> I see pieces of my wall
> Scattered all around.
> Here I am in the midst of them

I *was* broken, I *am* healing, and I *will* overcome.
Each piece has purpose and hope.
A foundation has already been laid
A firm foundation
One that cannot be shaken
And with His help we rebuild
He and I.
Each broken piece we bind together
One on top of the other
I see progress, hope
Instead of a wall
We build a mansion
I shall reside there
With purpose, dreams, and hope.

                --Susan Kocak

19

Cloud and Fire

It was a bad, bad decision. I'd been biking alone through Utah. Although that state has some spectacular landscapes, I was tired of doggedly pedaling alone through the desolate stretches. I just wanted to get the long, lonely stretches behind me. And so I made one of the worst decisions of my life.

Late in the day, I stopped at a small cluster of buildings along Lake Powell. Inquiring about lodging at the marina, I found there was none. The only suggestion was that I could camp on the shores of the lake.

I'd already ridden 100 miles that day, and I wanted a bed to sleep in. The next town was Blanding, Utah, on the other side of a mountain. But that was another 80 miles away. I could do it, I thought. I took off.

In that entire 80 miles, I only met one car, and that was early in the evening. The driver stopped to ask if I needed help. The idea of someone pushing through that stretch with night coming on was so outlandish that he assumed I must be in need of help. Otherwise, I wouldn't be out there.

I pedaled into the darkness. It was cloudy and so, so dark. The headlight on my bicycle failed. Two days of rain prior to this had apparently ruined the connection. I coaxed a feeble glow from the light, but it flickered and died. I'd squeeze and rub and shake it and would get a few more yards of light on the dark pavement. Finally, it died and refused to be coaxed or coerced back to life. The night was utter blackness.

Then the cold of desert night set in.

I was so, so alone. At one point, I could hear animals along the road but couldn't see a thing. Bushes and rocks took on strange, menacing shapes. I could barely see the white lines on the road. Then the incline grew steeper, and my strength was gone. I couldn't pedal, so I pushed.

Sadness and loneliness hung heavily over every step. No one knew I was out there. My family and friends did not know what I was going through. I had no idea where I was headed or what was coming next along the road or when this cold, dark, awful journey would end.

At about three in the morning, I collapsed and rolled into a ditch and slept.

Perhaps you're slogging along in just such a journey? So alone. No light guiding your way. Exhausted to the point of giving up. Not knowing when or if you will ever find comfort. Lying in the ditch because there's nowhere else to rest.

Look up! There's a pillar of fire up ahead!

Can you hear the whispers among the former slaves as they move out of Egypt?

Where are we going?
I don't know. Outta here. Following Moses.
Does he know where he's going?
He's lived in the desert the last 40 years. I hope he knows.
The desert? We're headed for the desert?

Remember, they had lived as slaves in Egypt, and before that, their nation had enjoyed dwelling in Goshen, some of the richest, most fertile land in the country. Now they're walking into a desert.

So it must have been an amazing sight when a cloud appeared that constantly moved ahead of them. At night, a pillar of fire guided them if they were traveling or stood guard over them in camp, giving them warmth and illuminating the cold desert night. Sometimes the cloud moved behind them and came between them and their enemies. The cloud and the fire were constant reminders of their God's guidance, provision, and protection.

Wouldn't that be wonderful to have such spectacular guidance and protection?

We do!

We may feel as though we're groping our way through darkness as black and lonely as my night ride through the mountains of Utah, but God promises us that He is here on this journey with us. He is providing for us. He is leading us. I know it doesn't *feel* as though He is here, but He is.

> In your unfailing love you will lead the people you have redeemed. In your strength you will guide them to your holy dwelling. (Exodus 15:13)

> "Because of your great compassion, you did not abandon them in the wilderness. By day the pillar of cloud did not fail to guide them on their path, nor the pillar of fire by night to shine on the way they were to take." (Nehemiah 9:19)

Our God is the same God, who will not abandon us in the wilderness but is always leading us home. Psalm 139 tells us He is with us everywhere we go, and this darkness we feel is not darkness at all to Him. He still has us by the hand. Psalm 23 declares that even though I walk in the shadow of death, He is with me. "I will fear no evil." With the comfort of our cloud and fiery pillar, we can say, "I will fear no valleys on this journey."

That cloud and pillar of fire were always there as the children of Israel traveled. So how could the people have forgotten that God was with them? How could they have doubted? All they had to do was look up and see the evidence that the living, almighty God was leading them and providing for them. How could they have panicked and gone back to worshipping the idols they had grown accustomed to in Egypt?

They did forget. They doubted, and they reverted to worshipping idols, hoping for the favor of "gods" who could not help them.

They forgot to look up.

Isn't that what happens to us? Our eyes are down here at earth level. We strain to see through the darkness. Black shapes rise up and alarm us. We feel so alone. We have no idea where we are or what road we should be taking. We start to feel helpless and desperate.

Have we forgotten the cloud and the fiery pillar?

During the summer and fall after the breakup with Her, I was a desperate man. I spent many mornings looking for the cloud to guide me. As a result, healing was coming. I wrote a book about it. And at one point I thought, *Okay, I've got it. I understand. I can do this now. I can do it on my own.*

I forgot about keeping my eyes on the cloud and the pillar of fire. And in a few months without that guidance, I fell into a deep pit.

Do we ignore His presence and leading?

Where are we looking for guidance?

Do we think we need other gods to get us through this?

It's worth taking some time to ask ourselves if we have run to other idols for comfort, relief, or courage. If we have, we'd better get our sights back on the fiery pillar and the cloud.

You will probably not see an actual cloud leading you along on this journey or a pillar of fire comforting you in the darkness. But you will see evidence of God's presence and His care for you along the unknown path you follow and in the deepest night. As you intentionally look for those confirmations, you will begin to see more and more of them, like comforting beacons along the way.

God is very intimate and personal in guiding His children. He guides through His Spirit, who has come to dwell within each of us. He came to live with us as a guarantee that we belong to Him, and He is our connection to the Almighty Father. Jesus said the Spirit would be our Comforter and Counselor who would teach us and guide us into all truth.

The Holy Spirit is the Guide who takes us down the paths that lead to restoration. We can be assured that Presence is always there because of His love and compassion. Always leading. Always providing.

I know it doesn't feel like it. It may even feel as though God has forgotten about you. Or that He has decided to let you flounder on your own through the hard consequences of your bad choices.

But He hasn't forgotten. He has not left you alone. Jesus said to His disciples back then and to His disciples now, "I will always be with you, right up to the end of time." He is the Great Shepherd, who keeps track of every one of His flock, knows what they're going through, and provides all they need.

In the darkest of nights, in the loneliest places, the cloud and the fire are there. In pain or rejection, in devastation or pandemic, in loss or in earthquakes that shake your world, look up and see the presence of the Great Shepherd in your life. He's constantly with you, providing for you and guiding you home.

20

The Master Workman

The house in Florida where Marv and I toiled for two months did not restore itself. We had a plan, and we applied sweat and muscle to achieve the vision of a new home.

God is the Master Architect who has planned our restoration. Yes, I know. Right now, it's difficult to catch the vision. You wish He would share more of the plan with you, or that He'd hurry up and get the job done. I am well acquainted with those feelings. But Isaiah reminds us the Lord has our well-being at heart and has plans for our restoration: "Yet the Lord longs to be gracious to you; therefore he will rise up to show you compassion… Blessed are all who wait for him!" (Isaiah 30:18) I'd certainly like to be blessed. But it is hard to wait. We want this journey, this restoration and renovation job, to be done.

Just as the house didn't renovate itself, we cannot do this hard work of following the Architect's plan by ourselves. We just don't have the wisdom, power, and strength within us. The Holy Spirit is here as our Helper. He will be our power to complete this journey of inward restoration.

The Spirit is the Master Workman, rebuilding the crumbled debris into a mansion. Be assured, He is at work. He's busy knocking down walls, clearing out debris, and rebuilding the new. And to be honest, only He can rebuild and create a mansion for me. I cannot do it on my own. You cannot do it on your own. Although the signposts on this journey to restoration are helpful aids to us, the miracle journey is not based on what *we* can do. The journey to restoration is possible only because of the goodness and kindness of our God.

There are times, as I sit on my porch and read the Word, that I get goosebumps when I realize what we have available to us in the Holy Spirit. The Spirit is at work changing us, and it is the Spirit who gives us new lives and the power to live those new lives. I am almost embarrassed right now, as I realize that I have the Holy Spirit within me and He has the power to get rid of this dead body that is still hanging onto me.

The Scriptures speak of our being "made new" and that we are His *masterpiece, handiwork*, and *workmanship* (Ephesians 2:10, various translations). The word *masterpiece* brings to mind a painter, laboring over every detail of the one painting she considers the height of her talent. You can use any example of an artisan's workmanship. For example, a baker who creates with great care and attention to detail a magnificent wedding cake. Or think of someone restoring an antique car or designing an heirloom quilt. Whatever the handiwork, the creator is constantly thinking about their work, laboring over every painstaking detail, intent on creating their masterpiece. That is how God labors over His own masterpieces.

It is the Spirit who creates a new "me," a masterpiece.

> We are being transformed into his image with ever-increasing glory, which comes from the Lord, who is the Spirit. (2 Corinthians 3:18)

> But when the kindness and love of God our Savior appeared, he saved us, not because of righteous things we had done, but because of his mercy. He saved us through the washing of rebirth and renewal by the Holy Spirit. (Titus 3:4, 5)

It is also the Spirit who gives the power to be the new "me."

> I pray that out of his glorious riches he may strengthen you with power through His Spirit in your inner being. (Ephesians 3:16)

> Walk by the Spirit, and you will not gratify the desires of the flesh. (Galatians 5:16)

You may feel painfully far from a masterpiece right now, but that is how God sees you and me. His kindness has given us the power and the tools. Will we open our toolbox and make use of what He's made available to us?

It is by the Spirit that we are changed and our lives are changed. Everything about our new lives depends on the Holy Spirit. Everything. He covers it all.

Last summer and fall, when I was desperately straining to hear God speak, I was so in tune with the Holy Spirit. As I walked on the trail and dialogued with God, He gave me such clarity of mind. From those times came chapters for *DWTL* like "The Stained-Glass Heart" and "The Alabaster Heart." Then, I grasped the power of the Holy Spirit.

But there have been days when I've looked around and wondered, *Jesus, where did you go? I don't feel anything...*

Regardless of how you may feel right now, He is always working. When we sit in the prison. When we're tearing down walls and rebuilding. When we stand bewildered in the wilderness because we've gotten confused and don't know which way to go. He is at work.

A Chrysalis Time

Have we wasted years of our lives?

All those years during which you worked so faithfully at that job, only to be told you have a few hours to clean out your desk. All that kindness you put into building a relationship with your neighbor, only to have him viciously turn on you. All those sacrifices you made for that kid, only to have him walk away from home one day and cut off communication with you.

I kept looking back, thinking, *Man, you've wasted a lot of years of your life. First the two years with Her. Then almost another two years on this journey through the wilderness.*

But is our time in the wilderness wasted?

God knows me well, and He knows that I learn the hard way. Because I've been my usual thick-headed self, He's taken me the long route to the land He promised me.

When the Israelites first left Egypt, they could have taken a much shorter route, but God knew all about them and about that highway—the emigrants would surely meet up with the fierce, hostile Philistines, and those natives would not be hospitable or helpful. I imagine that the people Moses was leading didn't even know how to fight. They'd been in Egypt 400 years, first protected by Joseph's influence, then as slaves. They had no army. God knew that they weren't ready for that battle. (See Exodus 13:17)

We think our lives must follow a certain route, but how many times has God saved us from battles that our faith is not ready to fight?

But where did the cloud and pillar of fire lead them? Back towards the Red Sea. And we know what happened there—they were trapped by the pursuing Egyptians. When the people saw the army chasing them, they panicked and turned on Moses. "Why did you bring us out here just to die? Didn't we tell you this would happen? You should've just left us alone in Egypt."

God assured Moses that He was planning something that would show both the Egyptians and the Israelites His power and glory. "Then they will know that I am the Lord!" Exodus 14:31 tells us that after the Israelites had crossed on dry land, then saw the waters sweep away the Egyptians and the dead bodies float along in the current, they were indeed in awe and put their faith in the Lord.

Can we trust that God has a plan and that He knows what He's doing as we journey through this wilderness? Will something good come from all this pain?

I'm not yet at the point in this journey to know what all God is doing in my wilderness, but a few things are beginning to emerge from the fog of my misery.

One is that God is humbling me and testing me to see what's in my heart and character. This was also one of His purposes for the Israelites' years in the wilderness (see Deuteronomy 8:2). For me, this was partially a disciplining by my Father (more on that later). God is bringing me to humility and to a total reliance on Him. This journey is so painful; I often wish for those wings of a dove to fly away. But if I do, I'll miss the journey of humility and arrive at the Promised Land and still be an arrogant fool. God hates arrogance; He says He can use the humble but He will destroy the arrogant. It was pretty important that I learn humility.

Could your loss actually be a blessing in disguise? Can a blessing come out of devastation? I had so many questions for God as I hiked the Appalachian Trail. Why would He take Mary? Why at that time, just as we were preparing to exit our jobs and do things like mission projects and volunteer ministries? Why did He not honor Mary's steadfast belief that He would heal her? Or did He honor it?

But because of Mary's death, I wrote a book, met many other people who struggled through grief, and was able to point people to Jesus. If she had not died, I may still be at the restaurant, making money, chasing other goals. I've gone from piling up treasures on earth to piling them up in Heaven.

Can good come out of devastation? Yes, it can. We don't wish for the pain. But I believe that someday I'll look back on this journey and thank God for it.

Another thing that is becoming clearer is that in the wilderness, God prepares us to do great things. Sometimes we look at others and think they've never had a wilderness experience. We feel envious of that. But if we look at God's Word, most of the great people who did great things went through a wilderness experience. The more intense their wilderness experience, the greater they were blessed and the greater was their work. In his wilderness, Job was stripped of everything in his life; then he was blessed with more than he had before. Peter went through a great wilderness as he realized he had abandoned Jesus and even lied about their friendship. Can you imagine his pain? Yet he became a great leader in the early church, preaching and bringing thousands to Christ and having the power to do miracles. His letters contain reassuring words for those going through suffering and struggles. Saul, after his meeting with the Lord on the Damascus road, spent three years in a wilderness retreat before becoming a missionary. Jesus came back from His wilderness testing prepared for His ministry and "filled with the Spirit's power" (Luke 4:14).

Desolate, painful deserts seem to prepare us for something else. If that's true, God has something great for me to do yet. While we are just trying to survive the grief, His plans for our tomorrows are already in motion.

Actually, the story isn't just about our days (or months or years) in the desert. While we are in the grip of this grief, it seems as though there is nothing else to our story. This devastation, this grief, *is* our story. Everything else dwindles in its shadow. But this wilderness is only a part of the much bigger story—our journey home to eternity and our final, ultimate salvation. God is leading His people home, and Proverbs 16:9 reminds us that we plan our course, but God determines our steps. Doesn't that change our journey if we believe that God is guiding us as surely as if we could see a column of fire or a cloud going ahead of us?

Maybe the reason God takes us on the longer route to restoration is because He wants us to become more like Him. That's part of the Spirit's work in our lives. Ephesians 4:24 tells us that our new selves are "created to be like God, in true righteousness and holiness." Created to be like God! How far along are you in that process? I've got a ways to go. It's not something we do ourselves, though. The Spirit is the one who is changing us, as we get to know our Father better and better (Colossians 3:10). That's our Father's plan—to change us to be more like Him.

My wife loved monarch butterflies. She'd gather the caterpillars, keep them in jars, feed them, and watch over them as each transformed into a chrysalis, a small green casing tightly holding the caterpillar within. For a time, the chrysalis hangs immobile, looking lifeless. But inside, a miracle is happening. The time comes when the walls of green become thin and translucent, and you can see the beautiful orange and black markings of a butterfly within. Soon, the butterfly emerges. Within that chrysalis, there's been a complete transformation from worm to regal monarch.

I liken this time we're in to a chrysalis time. That's more hopeful than calling it a desert experience, isn't it? But here's where our hope lies—in God's power and process of transformation. We're held tightly in the chrysalis right now, but God's power is at work, and the time will come to break out of the chrysalis, transformed.

There's a major difference between us and monarchs, though—their time in the chrysalis stage is usually only 10-15 days. Me, I'm taking a bit longer in the transformation process. But my hope is in God's power to change a worm into a butterfly. When I do get to the place God wants me to be, I'll fly and soar into the Land of Promise.

I gave my heart and trust to someone and expected that it would be treated kindly. Instead, it was shattered. The loss was devastating to me. What I really want now is someone I can trust completely, someone who trusts me completely. I've asked God, "Can I trust You to send me someone who is trustworthy?" You see, even my trust of God has been shaken.

But the very thing I lost—trust—is what God is asking of me. He's asking me to trust my life to Him, to trust that He is not wasting time in what He's doing, and trust that He is leading my steps. Many times, Jesus said to someone He had healed, "Your faith has made you whole."

Can we wait for God's best for us?

Can we take the pressure of the chrysalis, trusting that even in this hard time, He is working His plan for us?

For the word of the Lord holds true,
and we can trust everything he does.
Psalm 33:4 NLT

22

Where's My Hope?

I had sent off that book of good memories and my open, heart-felt letter asking for answers to my questions. I thought those questions could be answered easily enough. And if She had enough compassion, she would answer so that I could heal more quickly. I wasn't trying to win her back. I just wanted to understand *WHY?* If She did care, she would want me to have peace and healing, right?

But there was only silence. No response came, and that set off a new cycle of wandering in the wilderness of pain and torment.

My hope for healing lay in getting answers from Her. And it wasn't happening.

The Israelites had not been out of Egypt very long. They were camped at Mt. Sinai in the desert. God called Moses to a conference on the mountain so that He could give Moses laws and instructions for this vast community of people He had chosen as His people.

Moses was on the mountain a long time. He was gone so long, in fact, that the people waiting below began to think something had happened to him.

Have you ever wondered why God has been "gone" so long? Or why He waits so long to PLEASE DO SOMETHING?

The people began looking elsewhere for help. They confronted Aaron, Moses' brother and second-in-command. "We need gods to go before us. Make us some," they demanded. They had spent centuries in the Egyptian culture that worshipped many gods, and now, with Moses' and God's apparent absence, they were reverting to that culture they had just left, thinking they had to worship and sacrifice to an array of gods and goddesses that ruled over life.

When we feel God isn't here for us or that He isn't going to help us or maybe even that He's too angry or disgusted with us to do anything about our situation, where do we go for help? Or maybe it's not even that we think God is absent. Maybe it never occurred to us to simply ask Him for healing. Perhaps we looked everywhere else first, before we even looked to God.

While Jesus was teaching on earth, He was besieged by desperate people who had heard He had healing powers. When they met Him, they had one request: "Lord, I want to be healed."

My healing was put on hold, stymied in the desert, because my hope was misplaced. I was counting on Her compassion, not on God's. I told Her, "I want healing."

God said, "I am the one who heals you" to the slaves as they left Egypt. He said to Jeremiah's people, who were being disciplined by their exile, "I will restore you to health and heal your wounds." Many prophecies speak of the healing that He will bring; a specific foretelling of Christ describes Him as arising "with healing in his wings."

My friend the psalmist King David knew all about the deep wounds of lies, betrayal, and duplicity. His laments in the psalms tell us of the anguish and grief he suffered from events in his life. One of the deepest wounds must have been having his son try to kill him and take his throne. How does one heal from such heartache? Yet he could also write in Psalm 103:

> Praise the LORD, O my soul,
>   [Amazing! He begins with praise]
> and forget not all his benefits—
> who forgives all your sins
> and heals all your diseases…

David must have been referring to much more than physical diseases, because he went on to write:

> who redeems your life from the pit
> and crowns you with love and compassion,
> who satisfies your desires with good things
> so that your youth is renewed like the eagle's.

What or who are you hoping will bring you peace and healing? What or who are you hoping will pull your life out of this pit you're in?

Look to the God of all hope if you want to be healed. Don't pin your hopes on the person who hurt you, or on your own ability to figure out all the answers, and not even on a book from some guy who has suffered a romantic breakup. Okay, I admit I write this volume in hopes that the guideposts I'm pounding out will be helpful to others who are coming down the same path. But the miracle is not in my words or in these guideposts. The miracle is in the compassionate kindness of our God.

As we pause by this signpost that says HOPE IS AHEAD, you might ask the question if there is any hope without God in the picture. My only answer is that I believe the only hope for me is in God. David expressed this in the psalms in numerous ways: "You alone are my hope," he wrote time after time as he sought God's help.

Depend on Him daily. He hears your lament, and He is there to help you.

The hope I see out ahead is only a mirage if God is not in it. It is God who can do miraculous new things in our lives. It is God whose guidance and provision enable us to go on. It is God who brings resurrection after death, builds mansions from rubble, and designs the miracle of a chrysalis. It is God who has given us a Spirit guide with unlimited resources. And it is God who can truly heal us.

23

My Only Hope

Ultimately, all my hope rests on one thing: the love God has for me.

Yes, I am trusting that His power can transform me. Yes, I trust in His promises that He is always there for me and that He works in my life.

But those all spring from one thing: His great love for us.

He might be a powerful God; He might be omnipresent and omniscient and be in control of the universe, but if He didn't love us, where would we be?

My sight is a little fuzzy as I read this signpost that says: HOPE IS AHEAD. I believe this is true, but my vision is limited at times. Still, my faith is going to keep trudging on, because I know a God who is emphatic when He says He loves me.

Jeremiah surveyed the devastation of his country, the misery of his people, and the bitter time they were going through. Then he wrote:

> Yet this I call to mind and therefore I have hope: Because of the Lord's great love we are not consumed, for his compassions never fail. They are new every morning; great is your faithfulness. I say to myself, "The Lord is your portion; therefore I will wait for him." The Lord is good to those whose hope is in him, to the one who seeks him. (Lamentations 3:21-25)

I was on the mountaintop for a while; then I got kicked off and tumbled to this desert valley. Whatever set you on this journey has left you battered, bruised, beaten, and rejected. The future is unclear and uncertain. Sadness and depression set in, we're confused and hurt, and we wonder where God has gone.

God is right here, holding you and me. Psalm 139 goes into detail: He holds us fast and His hand guides us.

I was taught that the proper place for a man to walk with a lady is on whichever side is open to the most potential danger. We walk between her and the street, or between her and the crush of crowds on a sidewalk. That's what I picture God doing—holding my hand, walking beside me as a shield against danger.

"But," you say, "He has allowed me to walk through this awful thing, this thing that destroyed me." We may feel destroyed. God says we are not. Believing what He says instead of our feelings—that's faith. He says He is holding us, and His love will keep us from being totally wiped out.

If I didn't believe in God's love for me, I might very well fall by the way on this arduous journey and simply give up.

Just as God provided for the children of Israel as they trudged through the wilderness, His love provides for you and me in our desert journey. Besides the guidance and protection He gave them, their clothes did not wear out, and their feet didn't blister or swell. He provided food and water—He "rained" down manna (Exodus 16:4). He fought with them when enemies came against them.

He not only gives us the promise of a land of restoration, He gives us promises for our desert journey. These are His mercies that are new every morning, as we trudge down the long, hard road.

> The LORD will guide you always; he will satisfy your needs in a sun-scorched land and will strengthen your frame. You will be like a well-watered garden, like a spring whose waters never fail. (Isaiah 58:11)

> The poor and needy search for water, but there is none; their tongues are parched with thirst. But I the LORD will answer them; I, the God of Israel, will not forsake them. I will make rivers flow on barren heights, and springs within the valleys. I will turn the desert into pools of water, and the parched ground into springs. (Isaiah 41:17, 18)

> I am making a way in the wilderness and streams in the wasteland. (Isaiah 43:19)

> Some wandered in desert wastelands, finding no way to a city where they could settle. They were hungry

> and thirsty, and their lives ebbed away. Then they cried out to the LORD in their trouble, and he delivered them from their distress. He led them by a straight way to a city where they could settle. (Psalm 107:4-9)
>
> The LORD will surely comfort Zion and will look with compassion on all her ruins; he will make her deserts like Eden, her wastelands like the garden of the LORD. Joy and gladness will be found in her, thanksgiving and the sound of singing. (Isaiah 51:3)

Streams in the desert, a wasteland blooming like Eden, a pathway being built—all of those things happen *in* the wilderness. Even joy and gladness, thanksgiving and singing! These are not promises for our destination, the land of restoration. These are promises for us right now, in the desert. They are expressions of His great love for us.

In many wilderness experiences, people feel rejected by God. Sometimes they see the Heavenly Father as a version of what their earthly father was. Their eyes are on people—who have disappointed them or, worse, done great harm to them.

Or you might feel rejected by God because bad things have happened to you. My wife, Mary, believed with all her heart that God had told her He would heal her. She died.

You might be feeling, as I have, that God is distant. You're out of touch with Him. Your relationship with God does follow the cycles similar to our human relationships—sometimes incredibly intimate, sometimes cool and distant. I know that many things can affect how I "feel" about my relationship with

God; just a lack of sleep or if we haven't talked enough lately can affect feelings.

And some of you might be so guilty and ashamed of what you have done and of what a rotten person you've been, that you feel you cannot even ask God for forgiveness. You may feel that He's punishing you for past sins. God says to you, "Jesus paid for all that. Every bit of it."

Then there's this black cloud that looms over us, the pandemic. We so badly want what we had before 2020; we want life to go back to what it used to be. Some people are being torn apart by the frustration, loss, helplessness, and uncertainty; suicide, depression, anxiety, and joblessness are becoming all too common.

What is the answer to all these scenarios? Realizing how much God loves us.

But how do we come to that realization? How do we sink our roots deep into God's love so that we're kept strong, as Paul wrote in Ephesians 3:17?

Let Him *tell* you. Read His Word. That's the central story of the Bible: God's love for us. Tune your ears to hear what He has to say to you. You'll find His love on page after page of the Scriptures. Look for more of His promises that you can hang onto as a lifesaver.

Let Him *show* you. Look for the cloud and the fire, for the streams and refreshing pools. Rejoice at every small bloom you see along the dusty road. Give thanks for the daily manna He rains down on you. Understand that each of those are a sign of God's presence with you and His care for you in this parched wilderness. Those things come from His love and compassion for you, the brokenhearted one He loves.

GUIDEPOST
↓ ↓ ↓

WEEP, WAIL, HOWL

24

The Breakdown Lane

A few weeks after the breakup with Her, I was in Florida. Traveling home, my thoughts were constantly on all I had lost, the excruciating pain, and my relentless questions.

I did think, though, that I was paying attention to both my speedometer and the accelerator as I cruised through Columbia, South Carolina.

Apparently, I was not.

All of a sudden, the flashing lights pulled up behind me. I eased over, stopped, and had an emotional breakdown—right there in the breakdown lane.

Tears were running down my cheeks when the patrolman came up to my window.

"Are you okay, sir?" he asked, upon seeing my face.

"No, I'm not," I managed to get out. "I just lost my best friend. Be kind to me."

As he went back to his car to write the ticket, I pounded the steering wheel and wailed and howled.

At one time, I would have looked at a meltdown like that and scorned it as weakness. But the truth is, grief takes your mind to the edge of sanity. A mind can only bear so much, and it's okay to weep, wail, and howl.

Ticket in hand, he returned to my window. He informed me I had been doing 85; the speed limit was 70. "I was kind to you," he said. "I marked you down as under 10. Just stay right here until you're ready to leave."

Grief bubbles up and takes over. You've lost a loved one. You've been cheated on. You've been fired. You've gone through a divorce. You've lost your "normal," pre-2020 life. You've lost your church. You've had to give up your most cherished dream. Maybe, you've lost your trust in God's love.

You have to grieve. It's necessary for healing to happen. You've got to slog through this. What you're feeling is normal.

I know it's painful. I know we go through a period when we try to deny the pain, but we must face and feel it. Emotional pain is worse than physical pain. I'd rather get beat up than go through the emotional pain of the last eighteen months. At times, we're blinded by the pain. We just long for it to end.

Go ahead, weep, wail, lament.

It takes courage to grieve.

I trusted someone completely, and that trust was broken. I wondered how I could ever trust again. I didn't only lose love. I lost dreams of the future. I lost relationships with a family I'd grown to love. I lost my sense of worth; I felt rejected and worthless.

Now the pain is slowly turning to anger. Anger is part of the grieving process, too.

I'm angry. At myself. At Her. Angry it happened.

The difference between losing a spouse to death and losing a spouse to divorce or a love to a breakup is that in death, the loved one is totally absent. In a divorce or a breakup, that person is still among the living; and often, they seem to be moving on, they're happy, they've got a new life, and you are not happy and you can't move on and your life has been shattered.

If I'm being totally honest, I wish a little bit of pain on Her. I hope that her new relationship has some bumps in it. I suppose people would say it's "natural" to be angry and to hope the person who has deceived you, hurt you so deeply, fired you unjustly, or taken advantage of you will soon "get their due." But I need to guard against those desires to be avenged. I want to be careful about what anger does to me. We can build prison walls out of the anger, bitterness, and unforgiveness—and next thing we know, *we* are the ones captive in a prison of self-pity.

The Bible says we're to be angry and sin not. It's okay to be angry; as a matter of fact, it's healthy and it's needed on the path to restoration. Just as we have to face the pain, we have to face the anger. If we don't, it will crop up sometime and somewhere down the road.

To be angry at the situation that happened to you is perfectly normal. So don't feel bad about getting angry about it. Anger is an emotional response. Be glad that you finally can be angry instead of just hurt, hurt, hurt.

But if I ask God to destroy Her and to demolish her dreams so that she would also feel some of my pain, that is sin.

I'm angry about how she treated me. I may have deserved it. I had done it to others. And I realize I share part of the blame. But that doesn't make it any easier. Why should I have all the pain? Why shouldn't She share a little of it? Oh… my human nature is coming through.

I'm trying to be angry without sinning.

Here are some things I'm seeing more clearly now, although the road is still a little hazy for me at times, blurred by the emotions.

Realize you aren't as strong as you think. Or, realize that you don't *have* to be as strong as you think you *should* be. You've suffered a terrible devastation. You've gone through immense loss. Grieving is not only okay, it's necessary if you want restoration after this loss. Every now and then, pull over into the breakdown lane and give in to that meltdown.

No matter how much of a mess we are, Jesus is still available for you and I to lean against. "Come to me, all you who are weary and burdened," He says, "and I will give you rest (Matthew 11:28)." Lay down that heavy burden and rest. He is the Shepherd who came to provide everything His flock needs, even in the struggles of the parched wasteland.

As you're sitting in the breakdown lane, peer through your tears. There's a sign up ahead: NEED HELP? DIAL JEREMIAH 33:3: "Call to me, and I will answer you…"

Collecting the Tears

I've spent a lot of time singing the laments David wrote. There's so much pain and distress in his words. Anger, too. At times, he instructs God: "Pour out your wrath on those who have wronged me!"

Then, so often, his lament turns on a dime, and the very next line goes back to praising God for His love and goodness. From anger and disgust to praise and gratitude, back and forth David goes.

Psalm 56 is just such a song. This was thought to be written during a time when David was actually captured by the enemy Philistines. They had a love-hate history. David and his band of followers actually lived in the land of the Philistines for a time when Saul was hunting him. They fought for the Philistines in their battles (except when the battle was against David's own people.) But now he's been betrayed, he's their captive, he's been slandered, "boldly attacked," and plotted against. His life is in danger. "Don't let them get away with their wickedness," David begs of God. (How many of us have prayed that?)

But twice in the short psalm, he shifts his focus abruptly and declares his trust in God and what God has promised. "So why should I be afraid?"

Here's one verse from that passage that struck me: "You keep track of all my sorrows. You have collected all my tears in your bottle. You have recorded each one in your book."

Okay, so tell me—how many tears have you cried this week? Maybe you didn't count the individual drops, but how about all the times you've cried? How many weeping sessions have you had?

I would imagine that for most of us who have gone through great pain, our answer is only, "Many. Too many to count." And sometimes I've wondered if God even sees my weeping.

But God knows! He's counted each salty drop. He's kept a record of all our sorrows. That reminds me of Jesus saying that God knows how many hairs are on my head. I have no idea. I don't even pay attention. But God does.

Your imagination might run with the idea of God having a bottle into which He's putting your tears. Or a book where He records sorrows and tears. But the message is clear: He's paying close attention to our grief.

> The Lord is close to the brokenhearted and saves those who are crushed in spirit. (Psalm 34:18)

He heals the brokenhearted and binds up their wounds. (Psalm 147:3)

So much emotion—both lament and joy—is evident in David's writings that we know he must have written out of first-hand experience. He knew about all the emotions of grief and joy, fear and trust, anger and faith, discouragement and hope. And these lines tell us that he had experientially known God's healing. He knew exactly what it was to have his crushed spirit restored by God's love and mercy.

Chapter 30 of the book of Isaiah starts out with these words from the Lord: "What sorrows await my rebellious children..." and the next sixteen verses detail the devastation that is coming to the nation of Judah. Their lives would be shattered like a piece of pottery. Then Isaiah says, "But the Lord's waiting for you to come to Him, so He can show you His compassion." Remember, these were people who had gone far astray from God, yet even then, He longed to help them and heal them.

God has seen every tear that has run down your cheek, my friend. He knows about the anger simmering inside you or the depression turning all of life a dull gray. He's keeping a record of your sorrows, every miniscule bit of the whole painful mess. He sees. He knows. He cares. And He longs to show you how much He cares.

TEARS

A sign posted on a bank vault.
My memory bank.
DON'T LOOK BACK
Memories once precious now so painful
Locked securely in the far recesses of my mind,
Stay back there.
DON'T LOOK BACK!
But memories are tricky little fellows.
They escape.
They know all the tricks.
DON'T LOOK BACK?
We will jump ahead.
Lying in wait they hide.
I stumble along.
Memories attack.
Give us our dues, they shout!
Alms,
An offering.
My tear container in Heaven is full.
The angels will empty it yet today.
See you tomorrow.

The Black Pit

Before I met Her, I was praying for love. The adventures of previous years, which you may have read about in my earlier books, no longer appealed to me. I didn't want to adventure alone. I wanted someone with whom I could share the experiences of life. I wanted to share with someone I loved.

Thus, one of my big questions for God has been, *If you gave me this gift of someone to love, why has it been taken away from me?*

The loneliness I battle now is ten times greater than the loneliness before Her.

I've gone through days, weeks even, when I've felt far away from all other humanity. Lost. Rejected. So far down that I had to reach up to touch the bottom. In the cold, slimy, black pit.

Loneliness is absolutely devastating. You feel as though no one knows what you're going through. No one cares. There's no shoulder to cry on because no one will understand.

Perhaps you've lost a loved one. Or you've been devastated by the actions of a friend you thought you could trust. You've lost a huge part of your life, worse than losing an arm or a leg.

Or maybe it's not that you've lost someone, but that whatever has happened to you has put you in such turmoil you feel battered in a stormy sea with no land in sight, no one to help you, no one who can truly say, "I understand," no one who really cares. Maybe no one even knows what you're going through.

My loss literally drove me to the edge of sanity. I hardly recognized myself during the lowest of the low times.

During one time of extreme loneliness as I dragged myself through the wilderness—okay, I probably wasn't even dragging, I was probably huddled under a bush with no desire to go on—a friend sent me this word: "The enemy is very good at using deep and painful loneliness to alter and relax our values, our beliefs, our standards. 'Anyone is better than no one' can sometimes actually feel true."

The enemy loves to use our loneliness. It's a powerful strategy. Be watchful for the lies the enemy so boldly puts in front of you: You're alone, but *everyone* else has someone. Everyone else is happy and pain-free; you know, because you've seen evidence of their wonderful lives on Facebook. You are struggling to take your next breath, but your ex is happily sailing on in life. The boss who lied about you and fired you has everyone convinced of the lie, and the truth will never come out. Your child ran away from home because you are a bad parent. You are going through this pain because God is punishing you and you deserve it.

Are you familiar with any of those thoughts?

If someone has betrayed you and left you in this pit, it's quite easy to fall for another strategy of the enemy: a wish for revenge. I mean, it's only *natural,* isn't it? It would only be *fair* if some of this pain settles back on them, right? Check yourself on that. Ask for the Spirit's help in the battle.

When the breaking and tearing of renovation in your soul has left you feeling cut off from human relationships, force yourself to seek out connections, however small. Aloneness opens the door for the enemy to slide in. I am fortunate to have sisters who love me, and they patiently listened to my grieving, A few good friends witnessed many of my tears.

The widow of one of my AT hiking partners invited me to join a group of friends for several days of hiking, biking, and socializing in Michigan. I didn't feel ready for such an event, but I went, and it turned out to be a special time that brought a balm to my soul. We hiked and biked in an area of gorgeous natural beauty, taking excursions through the little harbor towns and enjoying many conversations as we explored the woods.

A retreat in the West Virginia mountains with my sisters and their spouses brought back memories of times we had all been there before and She had been there, too. And yet, it was a good time of connection with people who cared about me. Instead of sitting at home alone, thinking, thinking, thinking, I was embraced in a household of people coming and going, playing games, talking. It was a time of healing.

If you see me writing poetry, you can be sure I'm either in love or in pain. It seems that's when thoughts coalesce into rhyme in my head. Or free verse. I've just learned about that form of poetry. At any other time, I cannot write poetry. But pain and love seem to bring the lines along and let them drop into my head.

Here's one short verse that I wrote when I was thinking about the Burma-Shave signs.

> While you walk alone
> Through the mist of grief
> Look up to Me
> For your relief

This is one thing I've found so important in the pit of loneliness. God is close to the brokenhearted. He sees all our tears and knows what has shattered our hearts. Don't look to social media or the world to tell you the truth about your situation. Look to Him.

Look to His Word. Paul wrote in Ephesians that the sword of the Spirit is the Word of God. He can use that sword mightily in your life. Yes, I'm certain you can find laments in the psalms that fit your sadness and pain, but we also find promises of hope and restoration in the Word. We're reassured of His constant presence, and His presence transforms loneliness.

There's an old story about a rabbi explaining to his students why Proverbs 6:21 tells us to put God's Word "onto" our hearts. Shouldn't we keep the Word "in" our hearts? (One modern translation does use "in," but most keep the word "upon" or "onto.") The rabbi explained that it is because our hearts are hard and sealed shut; we often are not ready to receive the Word *into* our heart. But when we place the Word *onto* our hearts, one day when the heart breaks, the Word will fall in and take root.

I've experienced that. The Spirit *does* use the Word. Put the words of God onto your heart.

A friend wrote this for me one night when loneliness was especially heavy on my soul:

> Just lonely
> And me
> Seems he's around a lot
> Always by my side
> Wanting to hang on
> He's a heavy burden
> I can't seem to shake
> A cold wet blanket
> A dark threatening cloud
> Of gloom
> He has almost become
> A part of me
> But for God...
> In my despair
> He is there
> His presence comes
> He knows my pain
> And cries with me
> He wraps me in His comfort
> Goodbye, lonely,
> I don't want you anymore.
> —Susan Kocak

27

Breaking, Boiling, Squeezing

As I worked in the house in Florida, I kept thinking that I was like that house. I was in sad shape, in desperate need of a restoration. But before Marv and I could restore and build new, the house had to be broken down and cleaned out.

In your house that needs to be restored, is there something that you're just not willing to tear down? Is there a closet there, a wall here, that you are unwilling to give up and demolish?

If you're like me, the answer is probably yes.

There are walls in my house that are fighting demolition. They are reinforced concrete. I think I know subconsciously what's inside each wall, although I can't verbalize it right now—or I don't want to name it. But I admit there's something there that I know still needs to be attacked with a wrecking bar.

In biblical terms, there's still some fleshly thing that has to be crucified. It's hard to get rid of. I know. We may think we've taken everything to the cross of Jesus, but the next day, we find it is still alive in us. That's why Jesus said we'll have to take up our cross *daily.*

I know God is working in me (like I worked in that house) and His finished product will be my redemption. A restored house, a restored me. But I also know there's something in me that is resisting the breaking away so that the new can come.

My grandson Blake has a hover board. Being of a different generation, my first thought when I saw him sailing along on the board was that it was something out of the movie *Back to the Future.* But as I watched, it seemed simple enough. All it required was a little balance and learning how to control direction. I should be able to do it.

I tried it in the driveway but was baffled by one thing: "How do you get off this thing?" I yelled.

"Just step off," came the instructions.

My brilliant idea was to jump backwards. I landed on my back on the concrete, and the back of my head smacked the hard surface. My son thought I'd killed myself.

After a blow like that, you'd think I would have at least a crack in my skull. But my head is so hard that the outer shell protecting the inner works held.

I think it's difficult for some people to be broken. I'm one of those people. As sentimental and emotional as I can be, there is still something in me that resists a deep, inner breakdown of things that really need to go. It's so hard.

And I know that if you are weeping, wailing, and howling, the last thing you want to hear is that we *need* to be broken, that there is purpose in our brokenness. But if we are not broken, there can be no growth, no good that comes out of our misery.

Last year, I had a mini stroke. After consultation and tests, the doctor prescribed a cholesterol medication. I took it faithfully but was dismayed at one side effect. I was noticing quite a bit of pain in my joints.

During a book signing at a restaurant in Florida, I had a conversation with an elderly man (at least, he was older than I was) who had experienced the same side effect of the medication. A friend had advised him to eat oat bran. He tried it, and found that it lowered his cholesterol and eliminated the need for medication.

I thought to myself, *Well, when I get back home to Ohio, I'll give it a try.* But at the same time, I knew that I probably would never get around to buying oat bran.

But...

That old man left my book table and went back to the restaurant gift shop. He returned with a small bag of oat bran. "Here," he said, presenting it to me. "Try it."

There was a lesson for me. The man had shared helpful information; I could have come home and implemented that information, but I probably wouldn't have gotten around to it. He changed the course of events and influenced my life by caring enough to give me a small gift. I'd never met him before and will probably never see him again. But he cared.

The package of oat bran was stored in my backpack for the next two months in Florida. Finally, when I returned home to

Ohio, I unpacked my things and decided to use the gift. The first cupful I mixed up was too watery. I did my Internet research and found a better way to prepare it. I also discovered I was actually eating too much of it. Only a quarter cup a day is recommended. Now I'm consuming a half cup. I boil the water, mix in half a cup of oat bran, stir briefly, top with blueberries, and crown it all with drizzles of pure maple syrup. Add a touch of cinnamon, too. This makes a tasty lunch for me, and it's packed with nutrients.

But you know what? For all of those nutrients to be available for use by my body, the hard, inedible outer shell of the oat grain has to be broken open and discarded. It is only the interior (the *groat*) that is processed and able to be digested.

A seed planted in the ground must also go through a breaking-open process for the seed to develop and produce all it was created to produce. In its bed of soil, that little seed must have its outer layer broken by moisture for growth to occur.

Whether it's a seed breaking in order to grow or a grain being milled so that we can benefit from its nutrients, that outer layer—the shell, the tough exterior—has to be broken.

My outer shell has to be broken. The hardness that is inhibiting my growth needs to be softened up and even destroyed for growth to happen. Whether that resistant, protective covering around me is self-centeredness, pride, stubbornness, or arrogance, it must be broken open for God to be able to use me.

We've used many metaphors here. They all point to one thing: This brokenness we're going through is necessary, not only for our healing but for restoration, availability to God, and growth into whatever He has planned for us.

One more example: the red beet.

As a kid, I loved to harvest things that grew underground. I'd pull or dig them, savoring the discovery of fully matured vegetables. Digging potatoes was like digging for treasure, and finding an especially big spud was cause for jubilation. The red beets would be pulled, their tops cut off, and Mom would boil them—for a long time, because the exterior is so tough. Once the boiling was finished, the beets were plunged into cold water. Then came my favorite part. I could grab that vegetable and squeeze it, and the outer skin just popped right off. The beet itself was full of nutrients. Sliced and browned in butter, it was as good as candy.

I'm a red beet with a pretty hard exterior. At least, I was. I've been boiled quite a while now. I'm hoping that God doesn't have to squeeze me too much before the good stuff pops free.

28

Crushed, Satisfied

The apostle Paul nailed it when he said that most of us would not be willing to die for another person. We even try to avoid being broken, crushed, and beaten up emotionally. We resent the pain. And if our devastation is caused by another person who has wronged us—well, that makes it all the harder for us to bear.

But we roll through Isaiah 53 (because we've read it so often we could almost repeat it without the page in front of us), and we completely miss the pain and brokenness of Jesus.

It took me many years to even begin to comprehend that Jesus was truly a man like me. Yes, he died on the cross, but he was God, after all; he could handle the pain, he can handle anything, right?

Then I hiked several weeks in Israel, and I walked the streets where Jesus played as a boy. I sat on the shore of the Sea of Galilee, and I could see him walking along and talking to his friends or sitting in a boat bobbing out there on the water. I stood on one of the mountains where he might have gone to pray after an exhausting day. I wandered the busy city of Jerusalem and thought about Jesus coming there to the Temple. On Israel's soil, I finally began to know Jesus the man.

Hebrews 4:15 reminds us that Jesus was a human just like us; he can empathize with us in everything we go through because he faced all the trials we face.

One of his first preaching engagements was in his hometown, and it caused such an uproar that a mob tried to kill him! Those were the people he had known all his life, his neighbors, childhood friends, and probably even some relatives. How would we handle such violent rejection?

He was tempted to wish revenge on those who mocked him. Actually, we are given a glimpse of a scene where he was tempted not only to *wish* revenge, but to bring it himself. When he and his disciples were traveling, they were refused lodging in one town. James and John were especially furious. They suggested Jesus call down fire from Heaven to destroy the town. His close friends brought the temptation, suggesting revenge.

During the years he was an itinerant preacher and crowds were gathering wherever he went, the time came when his family decided they needed to do something. It was obvious that his mind was not quite right. Some people were whispering that Jesus had demons in him, and even his brothers did not believe the things he was saying—his own brothers.

His popularity soared for a while. People hungry for change fell in love with the possibility that he would bring some kind of revolution. But that love affair ended, and many of them ended up rejecting what he was really teaching because it wasn't what they wanted to hear. It was just too hard. They didn't want him and his talk of a kingdom. They wanted something else. They dumped him and looked elsewhere.

Oh, but Jesus had a handful of really close friends. One of them vowed he would always have Jesus' back. But when the moment of truth came, the betrayer was one of his inner circle; it was he who brought the soldiers to the place where he knew Jesus would likely be praying. After the arrest, all the other friends deserted Jesus, afraid for their own safety. The one who had vowed that Jesus could always count on him? That friend lied and denied their friendship.

Jesus came to his own people and was rejected. He was tossed aside. It was his own people who killed him.

We know he wept. He wept over the death of a close friend and he wept over a city that rejected him. The night before Jesus died, he spent hours in prayer. Face to the ground, he pleaded with God to spare him the suffering. But there was no other way. And he finally said to God, "Then so be it."

The final, most devastating blow for Jesus must have been those moments on the cross when he felt that even God had abandoned him. He had dedicated his life to God and God's plan, and at the moment he needed God the most, God turned His back. Can you imagine the black pit of loneliness?

I felt completely abandoned, forsaken, and rejected. Jesus knows what this is like. As a man on this earth, like you and me, he went through worse. Rejection. Abandonment. Loneliness. Suffering.

Jesus knows what it is to be devastated by human relationships. He knows the grief of rejection. He understands what we're going through because he went through the same things. My trip to Israel brought about a reciprocated understanding—I began to grasp more of what Jesus felt as he lived on this earth as a human, in human relationships and facing the brutalities of those relationships.

Those last words from the cross, "My God, why have you forsaken me?" hold so much pain. Isn't it the same question we've asked? *God, where are you in this? Do you know or care what I'm going through?* We know what this feels like, don't we? Jesus does, too. He knows exactly what we're going through on this journey.

Isaiah 53:3: He was "a man of sorrows, acquainted with grief." Despised. Rejected. Crushed. Beaten. And in the end, it seemed like his life had been wasted, worthless.

The one who came to save us. Broken. Devastated. Crushed. Rejected.

Then verse 10 shocks us: God's plan was to crush him.

At what point in his growing up do you suppose the young Jesus knew that this was going to be his mission in life? He had to be broken to save and heal us—he had to go through this for the sake of people who rejected him and hated him and treated him so badly!

This being broken for the sake of others—that's not what we would choose. We would rather not be crushed, not even for God's work. I think Jesus struggled with it even more than I am struggling now. I know I have to die daily. There are things in me that need to be crucified. I don't like the pain. But I have not sweated drops of blood as I agonize and ask God if there is any other way to get through this. I would prefer some other way, too, something other than being so broken and having to slog through this grief. 0f

But Jesus came to a point of obedience: "Thy will be done." Am I there?

Isaiah 53 does not end with the rejection, beatings, crushing, and agony. As a matter of fact, the very verse that says God's plan was to crush him ends as the chapter ends—with triumph: "the LORD's good plan will prosper in his hands" (NLT).

Jesus' journey was the greatest Miracle Journey. Isaiah 53:11 declares, "When he sees all that is accomplished by his anguish, he will be satisfied" (NLT). Romans 5 tells us what his suffering brought about: God's gift to anyone who wants it, a right relationship with Him, a new life, and triumph over sin and death.

Does my life, even in a small way, bring life to others?

Will my journey point to Jesus, who can change lives in such a big way?

NOTE:

You may have noticed a departure in this chapter from a personal rule in my writing. Normally, out of reverence for God the Father, Jesus Christ the Son, and the Holy Spirit, I capitalize pronouns referring to them. I did not follow that practice here.

Here, I wanted to write about Jesus suffering *as a human being*. He experienced all the feelings, thoughts, and temptations that we struggle with. Hebrews 2:17 says He had to be like us "in every way" so that He could be our high priest and offer the sacrifice for our sins. He knows our pain, not only because He's our omniscient God, but because He's felt the pain just as deeply as we have.

During my time in Israel, I began to know the human Jesus better, and it deepened my love and honor for the One who came to save me.

29

This Kindness

Hikes on the Appalachian Trail and the Camino de Santiago in France and Spain were in so many ways microcosms of our greater life journeys.

As I began both hikes, I was very aware that each decision I made changed the bubble of companions in which I would walk the next day. If I decided to take a day off the trail (a "zero" day), it meant I would be on the trail with a different mix of people the next day. If I put in an extra-mileage day, I might be hiking away from hiking partners who stopped earlier in the day; in some cases, I never saw them again. If I chose to hitchhike to skip a rough section of trail (which I never did, but it was tempting for many), I might be separating myself from people I'd shared the trail with for days before. Even the simple fact that I chose one day to start the hike, rather than the next day or the next week, determined who I would meet, the interactions I had, and even the weather through which I walked. Choices changed my hike.

As you and I trudge through this wilderness journey together, there is one choice coming up that will make all the difference in your journey. I know, because I can testify that this choice completely changed the journey for me. It was a smaller miracle on the larger miracle journey.

You will come to a fork in the road, and you'll have to choose which option to take. Or perhaps we don't choose. Perhaps our Guide on this journey is the one who gently pushes us along the way. Listen for His wisdom as you consider your choice, marked by two signs, pointing in two different directions.

One sign says PUNISHMENT.
The other declares KINDNESS.

When our lives have been shattered and we are left alone to survey the dried bones and the carnage of devastation, the road ahead is lonely and hard. Healing does not come easy. It's one small step forward, and then two giant steps back.

When another person has caused our pain and left us in pieces, it's natural to ask why *we* are being punished but *they* are sailing merrily along with no cares or regrets.

Or, if we are trying to recover from an event like the death of a loved one, a life torn apart by fire or flood, or the destruction caused by a disease, then we might be wondering, *Why is God punishing me?*

I had spent months wondering why I was being disciplined so harshly in this desert. Then came a revelation. I suppose it was that fork in the road with the two signs.

I realized God is taking me down the road of His kindness. He is treating me as His son.

> Because the Lord disciplines the ones he loves, and he chastens everyone he accepts as his child. Endure hardship as a discipline; God is treating you as his children. For what children are not disciplined by their father? (Hebrews 12:7)

We tend to think of this desert we're forced to navigate as a dry, barren, worthless land. But it's also fertile ground for our God to work in us to bring healing, knowledge, wisdom, love, gratitude—a bountiful crop He wants to grow in us.

Every choice I've made has brought me to this place in my life. The law of sowing and reaping is always in effect. But God is still guiding, and in every consequence or circumstance, He knows what I need and He's working to bring it into my life.

Just as athletes commit to the disciplines of training, diet, and rest to achieve their goals, so hard times as we travel through life are opportunities for us to develop the "muscles" we need:

> We can rejoice, too, when we run into problems and trials, for we know that they help us develop endurance. And endurance develops strength of character, and character strengthens our confident hope. (Romans 5:3, 4)

Rejoice? Really? Can we possibly rejoice in this hard, painful time? James opened his letter with almost the same idea, although he phrased it: "Consider it pure joy whenever you face trials of many kinds." He also affirms that testing produces endurance, and then he adds, "Let your endurance grow, so that you will be mature and complete, not lacking anything."

I'm onboard with the goal of being mature and complete, but I still am trying to grasp the *pure joy* of what I'm going through. My brain sees James and Paul's point, but my heart and soul have to travel a little farther along the path until they fully understand the joy of what God is doing.

What's happened to you in this pandemic? Have you shriveled up in fear and confusion? Or have you found your patience, your character, the fruits of the Spirit all growing larger in you? In addition to the pandemic, this country has seen great social and political turmoil, and 2020 has shown us what our character and our faith truly are—or aren't. Throughout all these months, we've had a chance to grow in character and faith.

The pain you and I have been through in our personal lives has almost destroyed us. But it can make us stronger. That's God's purpose in these consequences and circumstances we have to walk through.

I've enjoyed watching a show called *Forged in Fire* on the History channel. Bladesmiths create weapons like daggers and swords. The steel is first put into a red-hot fire to burn away impurities. Then it's pounded, pounded, and pounded more. As the process continues, the smith cuts away what he doesn't want and can't use.

I see myself there, in the fire, red-hot. Being pounded and pounded. Having things cut away. This has been painful. Nothing about this process is pleasant. And in all honesty, I have fought the Smith almost the whole way. I've lamented in my pain and grumbled to God that He could be quicker about this whole process, and He has said, *And you could be quicker about this, too, if you weren't so stubborn.*

Besides growing desirable qualities in us, God uses this process of testing and trial, this journey of pain, to burn out impurities and cut away what needs to go. My journey, it seems, has involved plenty of burning and cutting.

The man I'm becoming has lost some pretty bad things. I was a bit arrogant. Prideful. I know God needed to humble me. His Word makes it clear that He hates pride and arrogance, but He favors the humble.

Moses spent 40 years in the wilderness, basically in hiding because he had killed someone. He may have thought this wilderness life was his punishment for what he'd done. But God was busy preparing Moses for the huge task of leading the children of Israel out of slavery. Many years later, we're told, Moses was the humblest man on earth.

Joseph certainly went through many experiences that humbled him. He was a cocky, boastful young man. His jealous brothers sold him to slave traders. In Egypt, his life was a roller-coaster, first rising in respect and power, then being stomped on and sent to prison where he was forgotten for years. Things must have looked pretty grim. He couldn't have known what God had in mind. I imagine he learned humility. Finally, when he was in a position of power, he was able to give mercy and forgiveness to his hateful brothers.

Why does God want us to be humble? He hates arrogance. Arrogance creates the illusion that we don't need Him. We don't trust Him—we trust ourselves more! We're so full of ourselves, there's no room for Him. But He can use people who are willing to be humble.

I had always thought myself to be humble. Here in our Amish/Mennonite community, we've made this a hallmark of our religion. We're humble. We make it our "brand." But like so many brands, it's only meant to manipulate others' perception of us—and our perception of ourselves. Our living doesn't back up our brand.

God's looking for a true humility. He's looking for broken people. People who know He is the only hope for our world. People who know all good things come from His hand. People who trust Him above everything and everybody else. People whose weakness allows the world to see God's power at work.

Proverbs 11:2 is a key verse for me. Ever since I was a little boy, I've prayed for wisdom. Early in life, I became convinced that wisdom was the most precious thing to seek. This verse tells me that pride brings disgrace, but humility brings wisdom.

My humbling has been a hard, hard process. I've had to be brutally open and honest with myself and with others. God had to break through my false sense of humility; He broke me down.

I'm beginning to see that God loves me enough to do me the kindness of letting me sit in the red-hot fire long enough to burn out impurities. He is kindly breaking off and cutting away the stuff that needs to go so that I can become the person I was meant to be.

As God prepared Moses and Joseph, God also uses our desert times to prepare us for something. He wants to use us, and He knows what adding to and purifying and cutting away is still needed so that we are available to Him.

I grieved longer than I needed to because I kept looking back, lamenting my pain and wounds as some kind of punishment and sorrowing that I'd wasted almost four years. But God wants me looking ahead, moving into my future. He knows what's ahead for me, and He knows what I still need to be able to move into that future. His kindness not only told me to step into the future, His kindness has also been preparing me for it—He's been working and has had a hand in my life all along. I've been a slow learner, have dragged my feet, and have had emotional, mental, and spiritual blocks, but God has been kind and has not given up on me in disgust.

Neither you nor I would have chosen to go through this breaking and this desert journey, but the truth is, God is using it for His good plans for us. We can thank Him that we are making the journey now, while we still have a good future ahead of us. He is preparing us for greater things.

God is breaking me down. I don't know all His plans, but perhaps one reason is so that I can be a better messenger. In 2 Timothy 4, Paul said that nobody stood with him, everyone had deserted him. But he didn't hold it against them because God was on his side and gave him strength and the message was proclaimed. Perhaps through your loneliness and pain, through my loneliness and pain, we have a message to relay to a hope-starved world, and God is forging us as weapons for his use.

A journey of pain seems to come before blessing. Why, I do not know.

Is God humbling you to prepare you for something big?

Is there active obedience He requires of you? Then keep looking forward in faith.

As long as this journey through the desert lasts, remember this:

The LORD will guide you always;
he will satisfy your needs in a sun-scorched land
and will strengthen your frame.
Isaiah 58:11

GUIDEPOST
↓ ↓ ↓

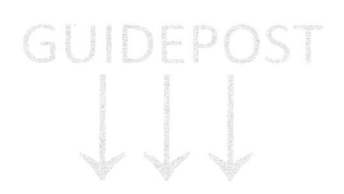

YOU NEED FORGIVENESS

30

Forgiveness for the Wounded

This will be one of the shortest sections of this book. The number of words on these pages is no measurement of the importance of this guidepost. In fact, this might be the most important section of our miracle journey.

These words are fewer simply because I am still learning, still trying to plumb the depths of forgiveness, what it means, what it looks like, and—the big question in all our minds—how can you possibly forgive someone who has hurt you so badly?

I said I forgave Her. I wrote it in a letter to her. But even as I penned *Don't Wait Too Long,* I could not get to the point of true and complete forgiveness. I couldn't.

Yet, is our forgiveness ever going to be *true and complete?* Can it be? We believe God forgives our sins completely. My hope rests on that. But He is God. Can we mortals ever get to that same kind of forgiveness? And if the answer is yes, how do we get there?

This I do know: I have to forgive. Jesus says I have to. If we don't, God will not forgive us. But my need to forgive is not only because Jesus commands it. My Guide, the Holy Spirit, knows I have to learn things the hard way, and He is teaching me that I have to forgive because *I need it.* I want to move on. I want to love again. Unforgiveness holds me back, keeps me stuck. I'm going to have to learn forgiveness by doing it. I'm not as far along in this part of the journey as I'd like to be.

Forgiveness is for the wounded, not the one who wounds. Whether or not She ever asks my forgiveness, whether or not she feels any remorse, I must forgive. For my own peace of mind and well-being, I must forgive.

Forgiveness does not say that the things that happened to you and me were right. Of course they weren't! Those events inflicted deep wounds that will leave lasting scars. What happened to you shattered your life—and probably other lives, too. The pain is real. What was done to you was wrong; in some cases, it's been pure evil.

There's the old lie that says we must "forgive and forget." No. There is no forgetting. As a matter of fact, without the remembering, there will be no forgiving. Forgiveness says, *I remember the wrong. But I will not hold on to the anger, the bitterness, the vengeance.*

Pursuing forgiveness is declaring the offence against me will not control me. It will not rule my life. This devastation will not control my thoughts and emotions; it will not imprison me.

As long as I'm angry at what She did and angry that I feel this way, I'm stuck. There's no going forward. *God, we're not getting anywhere.*

And there we have the answer: *God.*

The Only Way

Let's start with a question that might shock you: Is it possible that as Jesus hung on the cross and endured devastating pain, loneliness, and death he was unable to forgive those who had brought about this ugly death?

Hold your answer... We'll come back to that.

My sisters and I all get along, and we love being together, so it's difficult for me to imagine the dysfunctional family of Jacob. As a quick review: Jacob deceived his father, cheated his brother, and ran off to another country to save his skin. There, he fell in love. But he in turn was deceived and given the wrong sister in marriage. Back in those days, it was common to have multiple wives, so Jacob also later married the preferred sister, the one he first fell in love with. Needless to say, there was some jealousy and competition between the sisters, and that grew into a race to see which of them could give their husband the most sons. This included producing sons by giving their women servants to Jacob to father more children. In all, Jacob had twelve sons with four different mothers.

Not an ideal foundation for creating a happy household.

Joseph was the favorite son of the favorite wife. His father doted on him. That didn't sit well with the rest of the family. Then the boy had strange dreams about everyone else in the family bowing down to him, and he had the audacity to tell his brothers about the dreams. That really didn't sit well.

You can imagine the aggravation the other sons felt. The bitterness. The anger. And then to have to listen to the kid go on about those dreams! But can you imagine selling your brother to a slave trader? And then lying to your father and presenting evidence to prove the boy is dead? The horror of that is beyond my imagination.

Things went well for Joseph in the foreign land where he was sold as a slave. He was liked and respected by the man who bought him, and his life was on an upward track when lies and deceit suddenly plunged him once again into a hole—this time, jail. Hope flickered for a brief moment when another prisoner was released and promised to advocate for Joseph's release also. But that promise was forgotten, and surely it seemed to Joseph that there was no hope.

How often did Joseph think of his brothers and what they had done to him? Did he spend long days looking back as he lived out years in the prison? Did he have nights of weeping, wailing, and howling? Did he go through a breaking open?

We aren't told what was happening inside Joseph during those times. Something must have happened to him in those in-between years, though, because when he was finally face to face with his brothers and given the opportunity to accuse and condemn them for what they had done to him—and by then, he did have the power to take whatever vengeance he pleased—he instead returned good for evil and saved their necks.

How did he manage to forgive those brothers who had used him so wrongly and carried out such terrible deception?

Only God could have worked the forgiveness and mercy that was in Joseph's heart.

We aren't told much about Joseph's relationship with God. Instead, we see how it played out in his life. When there were visions to be interpreted, Joseph had the insight to do it. But he was quick to say, "Only God can tell you this..." When he reassured his brothers that he wasn't going to take off their heads, he said, "You meant what you did for evil, but God meant it for good."

Joseph knew God. For all those years in Egypt, during the good times and the really bad times, he must have held onto his belief and trust in God. We have one more amazing evidence of his faith... but we'll look at that later.

Without knowing God, is it possible to forgive such terrible wrongs? I cannot say; I only know that even when we do know God, it is hard for us to forgive deep wounds.

I know forgiveness has something to do with controlling your thoughts. That's not easy when you're devastated. All you can see, feel, and think about are the pain, the injustice, the abandonment, the betrayal, the loss, the impossibility of putting your life back together.

Is it possible that it was even difficult for Jesus to forgive? He was fully human. He had to live and die as one of us to pay the price for us (Hebrews 2:14-18). He had all the struggles we have. That surely includes this great struggle to forgive. He knows what we're going through.

I wanted Her to ask me for forgiveness. Oh, how I wanted that! But when Jesus died on the cross, he didn't wait for his accusers and executioners to say, "We're sorry we're doing this to you. Please forgive us."

However, he also did not look at those people and say, "I forgive you."

He said, "Father, forgive them, for they know not what they do."

Jesus asked God to forgive them. He didn't say forgiveness was his to give. Maybe as a human, he couldn't? Maybe he didn't?

In Acts chapter 7, we read the story of the stoning of Stephen. As he died, his prayer was "Lord, do not hold this sin against them." He, too, prayed for the Father's forgiveness of those who killed him.

What do these accounts say to us? Is real forgiveness only possible when God brings it about?

Romans 8:26 tells us the Holy Spirit helps us in our weakness. As an example, the Spirit takes over when we don't know how to pray, and He himself intercedes for us when our need is beyond our being able to express it.

When it comes to forgiving deep wounds, most of us find ourselves in the grip of the old sinful nature. It's hard not to hold a grudge. It's hard not to nurse and nurture our anger and bitterness. I mean, we're perfectly justified in these feelings, right? It's just natural to feel this way, agreed? Isn't it only fair that someone who has wronged us so deeply should somehow be paid back for the pain they've wreaked on others?

Except…

Except that Jesus, the one we call Lord, has outlined another way:

> "But to you who are listening I say: Love your enemies, do good to those who hate you, bless those who curse you, pray for those who mistreat you." (Luke 6:27-28)

This is how the sons and daughters God has adopted—Jesus' brothers and sisters—are to respond when they are mistreated. Other translations or versions use the phrases "those who hurt you," "those who abuse you," and "those who spitefully use you."

How is this even possible? Isn't this teaching too hard for us?

Yes. It is.

Our only hope rests in the Holy Spirit who helps us in our weakness. Our own nature is too weak to forgive. Our own nature wants vengeance! We don't want to let go of the anger.

I wanted to be able to pray, "Lord, bless Her." I wanted to. But I couldn't quite do it.

Only the Spirit of Christ who lives in me can do that.

Jesus dying on the cross and Stephen falling under the stones raining down on him knew the way to forgiveness. They looked to God, who holds the only possibility of doing the impossible.

32

Coconut Cake

This book is about recovering from pain inflicted on us, but my hope is also that we become more aware of what we do to other people through our decisions, actions, and words. Sometimes it is intentional, and we know exactly what we are doing. Sometimes it is entirely unintentional, and we aren't even aware that we have hurt someone.

If *you* have been the one who inflicted pain, I hope you know how important it is to ask for forgiveness and try to make things right.

Last year, when I went through all that pain of the breakup and realized that I had also caused other people pain over the years, I asked the Holy Spirit to remind me of anyone I had wronged. I wanted to ask their forgiveness for whatever I'd done to cause them pain. On the occasion of my leaving this earth, I don't want anyone to be saying, "He wronged me and never apologized or asked forgiveness."

"Anything, anything," I told the Spirit. "Show me anything I've done to hurt someone else. I want to make it right."

He did reveal things to me—actually, in most cases, He didn't have to reveal them. I already knew of wrongs I'd done and ways I'd treated people that needed to be acknowledged and forgiven. I called people and asked to meet with them. My repentance was sincere; I was frequently in tears as I admitted I had wronged them and said I was sorry and asked for their forgiveness. Often the response was, "I forgave you a long time ago, for my own sake." But I needed to ask forgiveness for *my* sake.

And then, the Spirit reminded me of the coconut cake.

My dad's family was Amish. Mom and Dad, as a matter of fact, were married in the Amish church and had a young family before they eventually decided to leave and join a Conservative Mennonite church.

The Amish community has long held the tradition of "shunning" those who leave their church. A shunned person is no longer welcome as a member of the community, and, in particular, they cannot eat at the same table as members of the Amish church.

My mom and dad, though, were never shunned. His dad was an Old Order Amish man who was a born-again follower of Christ. He was clear about his position: "I will not shun my children." And some of his children did leave the Amish; several of his sons became preachers in other churches. Two sons were ordained on the same night at two different congregations. Somebody asked Grandfather which service he would attend. "Neither," he said. "I'm going to be at home on my knees praying for them."

Dad worked in a feed mill, and an Amish boy who worked there was making plans to leave the Amish church. This young man's family, though, did believe in shunning, and so he could no longer live in his parents' home. Dad offered him a room downstairs in our basement, where we had a bedroom and a bathroom that became Eli's space and his temporary home. We still used a portion of the basement and walked up and down, back and forth, through it. Eli and my dad both had a sense of humor and enjoyed playing the guitar, and Dad became a mentor to the young man.

One day when Eli was at work, I went into his bedroom. I don't know why. I was young, but I was old enough to know better.

Eli had a stove in his room, and I opened the oven and my wondering eyes beheld one of those square Pepperidge Farm coconut cakes.

I love coconut. I remember discovering it at Grandma's house. She had a container filled with something white and flaky. Never having seen it before but intrigued by the look and the aroma, I scooped out a small handful. The moist flakes were the best thing I'd ever tasted in my life. I loved coconut. Those pink coconut cakes that Dad sometimes bought for us when I rode the feed mill truck with him had also become a favorite treat.

In Eli's room, I stood there at the stove and looked at that coconut cake. Oh my, did that cake look good. And it was clearly a *bought* cake. We ate homemade cakes at our house. Something about a cake bought ready-made intensified the appeal.

One small corner had already been cut out of the cake. I could see it was a vanilla cake with a soft, fluffy frosting that I knew would melt in my mouth. And it was covered with *coconut!*

It couldn't hurt to have just a taste. Eli had already cut off a small portion. He would not notice an additional thin sliver carefully cut off. I went upstairs and came back down with a fork.

Just a tiny slice. Just a nibble.

Yes. It was even more delicious than I had imagined.

One more insignificant, minute bite.

Mmmm, said one part of my brain.

You'd better be careful. You don't want him to see you've eaten his cake, said another part of my brain.

But oh, was that cake good. And it didn't seem right that I didn't share this treasure with my sister. She was the sister closest to me in age, and we often shared adventures. I went upstairs.

"Come taste this cake," I told her. She came, and she did taste.

Well, we kept nibbling away at that cake. Something inside me chanted, *I don't think he'll see it. Just one more tiny bite. I'm sure he won't know.* But my eyes watched as that small empty square kept growing longer and longer. I could see cake was disappearing, but my mind denied the obvious.

The next evening after Eli came home from work, our paths happened to cross.

"Say, Paul," he said with a knowing look. "I think there was a little mouse nibbling at my cake. You don't know anything about that, do you?"

"No, no. I don't know anything about it," I said.

First I stole. And then I lied.

That's how the devil works. "Just take a little sample of this. It's *not quite* a sin. It won't make a difference to anyone."

The straight and narrow path and the broad way run in very close proximity at times. The devil convinces you that you can walk on the broad, easier road for just a few strides and you don't have to feel too bad about it. Even if you do feel guilty, you'll get over it. And you do it again. And again. And you keep going farther and farther down the wrong road.

Well, the coconut cake caper was more than sixty years ago. Over the years, my sin occasionally came to mind.

During the time I was asking the Spirit to remind me of people I had wronged, I was at the local grocery and saw—you guessed it—a Pepperidge Farm coconut cake.

Yeah, you little mouse. You did eat some of that cake that wasn't yours. And then you lied to cover up your theft.

The devil tried to get his argument in. "It wasn't much. It was such a little bit of cake. You could probably just let it go. Forget about it. Eli doesn't know about it, and even if he did know, that was so long ago, he's forgotten about it."

But I wanted to make it right. I bought the cake that day and went out to Eli's house. Opening the box, I laid the coconut-covered square before him. He looked at me in wonderment. Why had I brought him a cake?

"That's to replace the little piece I ate out of your cake when you lived in our basement." I told him the story. He laughed and said I wouldn't have had to buy him a cake.

But I'd stolen from him and then lied about it. It was wrong, and I wanted to make things right... even if I was sixty years late.

I suppose my theft of a bit of cake did not cause Eli much pain. But we humans can hurt people deeply, much more profoundly than stealing a piece of their cake. Sometimes it's unintentional. Sometimes, we are aware that what we're doing is not right but we tell ourselves, "He'll get over it," or "It didn't really make a difference to her," or even, "It's unfortunate, but I didn't have any other choice." And sadly, sometimes we are purposely cruel.

Think about what you do to other people, how your actions affect them. If you've caused pain and inflicted wounds, ask forgiveness. This is a start toward healing and peace of mind—for both you and the person you've hurt.

33

Times of Refreshing

*Repent, then, and turn to God,
so that your sins may be wiped out,
that times of refreshing may come from the Lord.
Acts 3:19*

I also need to forgive myself.

As I've traveled along this road—before you came to walk with me and share the journey—I passed through a dreadfully rough section. Perhaps you've had to traverse the same section or one similar; perhaps this section still lies ahead of you. It may not be as rough as what I walked through, but it's probably there, somewhere, in everyone's miracle journey.

There was one week that I can only describe as *horrible*.

It was the week I met myself.

I had already written the coconut cake story. I had already urged readers to consider their lives and ask forgiveness if they were the one responsible for the pain. I had already written other lines imploring folks to consider the consequences of their actions, the devastation they cause when they do not act honorably. I had already gone back to people I'd hurt and asked forgiveness.

Then my mind went back even further, and I remembered the time ten years ago that I had done to another person exactly what She had now done to me.

I came face to face with myself and saw who I had really been in that long-ago situation. I had been Her.

At the time, I felt "right" about what I was doing. I had a plan. I had everything figured out. I was doing things the logical way—at least, it was logical and legitimate to my mind. Instead, it brought misunderstanding, frustration, and anger to another person. At the time, I thought that person was unreasonable and treated me badly. But now I see that I was the one who was wrong. I looked into the past and saw myself standing there, doing the same thing to someone else that She did to me. The very thing that now hurts me so deeply, I had done to someone else years ago. The fault way back then was mine, and mine alone.

When you meet yourself like that and you realize how you have failed and what you've done to others, believe me, there are tears, an agony of remorse and regret, and more tears.

This rough patch of the road we're traveling requires repentance and forgiveness. I need to repent of what I've done in the past, of the hurts I've caused, of my arrogance, and of who I was then. I need to forgive myself, too.

To see myself in the mirror, to realize that I was Her, was humbling. It broke me more deeply, more thoroughly, than the emotional pain I was already suffering.

I need to repent and forgive myself, too, for my part in the failed relationship with Her and for the feelings I've had toward her.

Anger is one stage of the grieving process. It took me a long time to get there, to get angry. Then I was angry at the situation, angry at the ways I was feeling, angry that She did it, angry at her subsequent silence.

I'd tell myself, *I don't want to be vindictive.*

Then, deep down, another voice said, *But I hope her new romance isn't going well. I hope someday she'll have to feel some of this pain she's put me through.* And when that voice spoke, I admit, it felt good—for a short time.

There is the constant battle between what the Spirit wants to do in my life and what human nature wants to do. I know I have not always chosen the right path. I know I need repentance and forgiveness.

Meeting ourselves, we'll have to take a close look and ask if we're also angry with God.

"You gave me this gift of love. Why did it end in such disaster?" I've asked God. I felt Him saying, *Exactly. It was a gift. What each of you chose to do with the gift was up to you.*

That led to my asking: Had I abused the gift? Even worse, had I failed God?

I grapple with the question of why God brought us together. I had first connected with Her when she reached out to me asking for help in writing a book. When we met and fell in love, it was the most beautiful thing ever, so powerful, so pure, so right. A spiritual romance, I called it. We both believed God was in our meeting. Now, I wonder if God had something prepared for us to do—write the book. But once the romance was in full bloom, we got totally distracted and no work on the book was ever done.

We failed. Did we fail God's plan? Is there a Plan B if we fail? Did we both fail to honor what God gave us?

Perhaps we need to repent of our anger toward God. This requires a deep, searching honesty. Have we been angry with God? Have we ranted to Him about the devastation that has shredded our lives? Doubtless we all have, and He can handle our ranting. As a matter of fact, He wants us to come to Him with everything in our hearts and minds. But under that rant or lament, has there been some subtle or not-so-subtle anger toward Him because He has allowed this to happen?

All of the choices I've made have brought me to this point. God allows us choices. And He often allows us to make unwise choices. As I grew up under my dad's guidance, he may have advised against some of the choices I made; he may have told me certain things were bad decisions. But he let me make the decision. And whether I showed good or bad judgment, I was still his son.

God advises us. He allows us choices. But even when we are unwise or downright foolish, we are still His children.

While hiking the AT, I sometimes took a wrong turn. When I found my way back to the white blazes, the trail never said,

"Hey, you wandered away, you're not welcome back, you don't belong here." No. It always welcomed me back and pointed me ahead.

God does that, too.

Sometimes we blame God for consequences we have brought on ourselves by our own decisions. I made choices. When I met Her and fell in love, I probably knew all along that it could end painfully. But I made the choice to keep going.

Everything I've done, good and bad, has brought me to this point. A broken man. Learning more humility. Now seeing that I've hurt people along the way—and repenting of it. God is getting me to what He wants me to be.

Without repentance and forgiveness, we're stuck. We have no peace. We go on hurting. And it's not the other person who is hurting us; when we hold unforgiveness, we are inflicting damage on ourselves.

Repentance and forgiveness—in whatever way is necessary—will energize and nourish us on our journey down the path God lays before us.

Be kind to yourself. Let times of refreshing come.

The high and lofty one who lives in eternity,
the Holy One, says this:
"I live in the high and holy place with those whose spirits are contrite and humble. I restore the crushed spirit of the humble and revive the courage of those with repentant hearts."
Isaiah 57:15 NLT

34

Daily, in Bits

Don't forgive too soon.

True forgiveness comes only after we have acknowledged the hurt and the anger. Take the example of a married couple who have had an intense argument and the husband has wounded his wife with words said. Ten minutes later, he is contrite, realizing how his words have hurt. He asks her forgiveness.

Should she say *I forgive you*? It would be more honest and real to say, *I will forgive you.*

I know this may sound odd, but real forgiveness comes in small portions over time. We cannot say, "I forgive you," and think that it's over and done, and forgiveness is accomplished. It is not. The work is still ahead.

To truly forgive, we must first recognize the wrong. We have to grieve. The hurt happened. Someone has shattered your life and left it in pieces. If we do not first feel the pain, then "forgiveness" is only words.

So don't forgive too soon. But don't wait too long to forgive.

When a gunman invaded a small Amish school in Nickel Mines, Pennsylvania, and shot ten children, killing five of them, the world was amazed as the Amish said, "We will forgive. We must forgive." *We will...* Forgiveness does not come automatically and immediately when we simply say words. It comes in portions as we *do* forgiveness.

Jesus gave us a picture of the process of forgiveness. Peter asked Him, "Lord, how often should I forgive my brother when he sins against me? Perhaps seven times?"

At that time, Jewish tradition held that one should forgive three times. I'm guessing Peter thought he was going well beyond what was required, so he was probably shocked when Jesus' reply was, "No, that won't do it. Forgive seventy times seven."

Some translations say *seventy times seven,* and some read *seventy-seven times.* The difference is in the translation—whether or not the Greek or the Hebrew is being translated. Regardless, forgiving 77 times probably seems as impossible as forgiving 490 times.

Notice that in this small scene in just two short verses in Matthew chapter 18, Peter doesn't say that the one who has wronged him is asking forgiveness. The question is only "How often should I forgive?"

Jesus' point is that forgiveness is a choice made again and again and again. Over and over. Coming in bits as we forgive daily. It's part of taking up our cross and dying daily to ourselves and being resurrected to the new life Jesus has given us. Daily we make the conscious decision to forgive and do things Jesus' way instead of the way our old nature would prefer to respond.

For most of us, if someone repeatedly hurts us, we would eventually avoid the person. Write them off. Reject them. Keep the toxicity out of our lives. Move to another state.

But Jesus says, "Forgive again and again."

What is forgiveness? Can you define it?

Forgiveness is very much like love. How do you define love? We go to 1 Corinthians 13 to see what love is, and we find that it describes what love *does.* (And by the way, one of the things it includes is, *Love does not keep a record of being wronged.*) All who have read that "Love Chapter" know the areas in which we are weakest; we know the things we struggle with, whether being patient and kind or always persevering or some other action of love. We are given a picture of what divine love looks like, how it acts—and that's how children of God are to love. It's a tall order, but we're promised a Helper.

When we try to define forgiveness, it is also better to describe what forgiveness *does.* Like love, forgiveness is not just an emotion or even a thought or mindset. Forgiveness is what we do, on a daily basis, with the anger and the hurt that has come into our life.

So what does forgiveness *do?*

> * Forgiveness makes the choice, again and again and again, even when the journey is long and exhausting.

* Forgiveness does not walk the same path as anger, bitterness, and vengeance. When these come alongside and offer *their* way, forgiveness refuses and hurries after the Spirit.

* Forgiveness does not ask for revenge to fall.

* Forgiveness drops baggage filled with grudges and resentment and asks Jesus to deal with it.

* Forgiveness treats the wrongdoer with 1 Corinthians 13 love and prays for them.

* Forgiveness opens the door and welcomes peace of mind and well-being. It releases from prisons of anger, and builds mansions of hope.

This is a tall order, too; but we're promised a Helper.

GUIDEPOST
↓ ↓ ↓

DINE DIVINELY

The Right Diet

No matter what version or translation of the Bible you read or in what language you read it, there's one universal language that we all understand: the language of food. We've been learning this language since the day we were born into this world and began to feel the regular and intense need for nourishment. Food speaks to people of every age, every race, and every religion. It speaks to our bodies, our minds, and our hearts.

Is it any wonder that God uses this language often in His love letter to us?

In Deuteronomy 8, we hear Moses addressing the children of Israel, looking back over their years in the wilderness and looking forward toward their settlement in the land of Canaan, the land of promise:

> "He humbled you, causing you to hunger and then feeding you with manna, which neither you nor your ancestors had known, to teach you that man does not live on bread alone but on every word that comes from the mouth of the LORD." (Deuteronomy 8:3)

On the refugees' journey from Egypt to Canaan, food was a huge deal. Millions of mouths to feed and traveling through a desert—where were they going to get food for this mob? Traveling for years, they were not going to be able to pack a lunch. Later in the journey, they found themselves traveling through countryside where those who dwelled there were hostile and unwilling to show any hospitality. And if you remember, food was one of the first things these travelers began complaining about.

The manna that arrived miraculously was not only to sustain them physically, it was also a sign of the spiritual sustenance provided by their great God. The instruction for manna-gathering each day was to gather only what was necessary for that day. Every day, new supplies would be sent. They were to learn to rely on God for divine dining that gave them life.

Jesus, modeling prayer for His disciples, told us to pray for our daily bread. Not weekly, monthly, or occasional bread, but daily bread. Daily we pray for sustenance that keeps us alive, keeps us going—physically, spiritually, and emotionally.

The prophet Jeremiah was not just a "weeping" prophet, he was also a reluctant one. In the days before Judah was devastated by Babylon, Jeremiah received this message from God:

> "Before I formed you in the womb I knew you, before you were born I set you apart; I appointed you as a prophet to the nations." (Jeremiah 1:5)

Jeremiah lamented that he was merely a child. "I don't know how to speak," he objected. Whether that means he really was a youngster or merely that he had no experience with public speaking and taking the role of a prophet, we do not know. We can see, though, that it was an excuse.

But the Lord reached out and touched Jeremiah's mouth. "I've put my words into your mouth," He said. "Don't be afraid of anyone. I will be with you and rescue you." Jeremiah would have reason to be afraid; the messages God gave him to deliver were scathing denunciations of Judah's evil ways and frightening warnings of God's coming discipline. Of course, such messages were not welcomed, and Jeremiah was often in danger.

In chapter 15 of Jeremiah's book, we are witness to a conversation between God and Jeremiah. By now, Jeremiah was well into his calling as a prophet of God, and people had not reacted well to his message. Jeremiah's words: "It would have been better if I'd never been born!" People hated him; he stood alone; and he begged God to step in and help him. "Punish my persecutors! Why do you let my suffering go on so long? Why don't you do something about this? Why doesn't my wound heal?" (How many of us have said similar words?)

But here's the line that spoke to me: "When your words came, I ate them; they were my joy and my heart's delight, for I bear your name, LORD God Almighty."

The path in life on which God put Jeremiah had been rough traveling. Yet God's words brought joy and delight. In spite of everything that he was enduring, Jeremiah had a divine dining experience.

I read that verse one day and realized: The right diet can change a person's life.

Anyone longing for joy and delight in their journey?

Seizing on that verse, I, too, began to eat His words. Some translations use the word *devoured* or *consumed*. I spent hours on the glider on the porch with God's Word, consuming it. Admittedly, I devoured numerous laments and complaints. However, slowly bits of joy and delight were beginning to creep into my journey.

In Revelation 3 verse 20, we hear Jesus say He is standing at the door and knocking. If anyone hears Him and opens the door, He'll come in and dine with us.

Let's pause at this signpost and consider its wisdom: DINE DIVINELY. Our souls need the nourishment; and beyond nutrition, aren't we all longing to have joy and delight back in our lives?

Life Essential

The hike on the Camino de Santiago in Spain is divided into thirds. The first third is in the northeast, over the Pyrenees mountain range; the second third is the high, flat central plains called the Meseta; and the third and last section is the hilly farm country of Galicia in the west.

Once I entered Galicia, I knew I was getting closer to the Atlantic Ocean. Fresh seafood is more readily available in Galicia, and one of the specialties of the area is *pulpo.* Octopus.

I like to try new things, and that includes new foods. So of course I needed to try this local food. In one little town, several of us hikers asked about a good place to eat octopus. We were directed to a restaurant, and we went in search of this dining adventure.

It was a small place. Immediately inside the door was a counter where a man had a big pot of water bubbling and steaming. We placed our order, and from the tank beside him, the man picked up an octopus by the head and dropped it into the boiling water.

When he deemed the *pulpo* ready, he plucked it from the steaming pot, held it up, and with a scissors snipping away, cut off the tentacles. The pile of octopus tentacles came to our table, a heaping plateful. Five of us ate from the heap of what looked like curly little pig tails.

If you haven't tried octopus, allow me to provide you with a vicarious gustatory experience. Imagine a plate mounded up with disgusting little worms. That's the visual. Force yourself to pick up one curl and put a piece in your mouth. What taste are you expecting? The best way I can describe it is to say it tastes like boiled rubber bands. The only difference is that if you boil a pot of rubber bands for dinner, the rubber bands will probably be tastier than the octopus was.

I did not dine divinely that night. I spent good money at that restaurant, but I consider it the price of the experience—certainly not the food!

God has a question for each of us. Yes, it was written about 2,500 years ago, but our God is the eternal God who does not change, whose purposes stand forever, and whose Word will outlast even the heavens and the earth. He asks this question of you and me now:

> "Why spend your money on food that does not give you strength? Why pay for food that does you no good? Listen to me, and you will eat what is good. You will enjoy the finest food." (Isaiah 55:2 NLT)

What have we been spending our time, effort, and resources on that does not give us strength? What have we been looking to in hopes of enjoying fine dining, only to be disappointed? What have we resorted to, looking for joy and delight?

Just as taking in good food does good things for our bodies, taking in the Word of God does good things for our souls.

Let's admit it: We eat some things only because we enjoy them; they might have nothing good to offer our bodies. As a matter of fact, in some cases, foods we enjoy tremendously are even harmful to our bodies. Then there are probably things you eat simply because you know they are good for you; you might force yourself to eat them, but there's no enjoyment in the eating.

The food God offers is both beneficial for our souls and a thing of delight.

Jesus said, "Do not work for food that spoils, but for food that endures to eternal life" (John 6:27).

When we're finished with this book, you will have read more Scripture quoted on these pages than in any of my other books. That's because I've found that my miracle journey depends on sustenance from the Word of God. That's where I found hope and refreshment. It's the source of wisdom, guidance, and power to deal with whatever we meet on our path. This signpost is an essential.

I'd grown up with the Scriptures being read at church, at home, and in my own personal time. I'd read the Bible cover to cover numerous times. But in the last two years, as I ate ravenously, starved for food that would satisfy my battered soul, many passages suddenly became more personal than ever before. God did have a feast prepared for me in the Word. Divine dining. The finest of food. The most reliable hope.

As Moses addressed the people toward the end of their journey, he reminded them that God had given to them His own words, "and they aren't just idle words—they are your life" (Deuteronomy 32:47, paraphrased).

Our Creator has given us His words, and they are life to us.

We can't make the journey without sustenance from Him. Miss this signpost, and I fear for your journey.

Cabbage Manna

Remember that long night I pedaled and pushed a bike through the misery of the Utah desert? I rode all night because I could not find a place to stay. The ride was lonely and worrisome. And so, so dark. I saw no other soul on that deserted stretch of highway.

My mind went many places during that long night. The loneliness brought back memories of my family and good times of my childhood. Memories of family are often tied to food. Or, perhaps, memories of food are tied to family. I was really hungry during that long night, too, so memories and food, family and food, family and memories—it all swirled together during the long, exhausting night.

One of my food-and-family memories is of snacking on cabbage. Every year, we'd make a trip to the Columbus zoo. That trip always involved candy and cabbage.

For at least a month before our planned trip, my three older sisters and I would "save" candy. If we had the good fortune of getting two pieces of candy, we'd put one piece in a special box, saving it for our trip to the zoo. We each had our own box (I kept mine on a shelf in the closet), and we never stole from each other. I also never touched my stash, unlike my sisters who would make frequent visits to their cache to eat some of the candy they had saved. When the day came for our trip to the zoo, we'd take our candy boxes along—and mine was always much more bountiful than my siblings'.

The other snack we loved was cabbage. Mom would send one of us to the garden for a head of cabbage, she'd slice it and pack it up to take along on our road trip. With a little sprinkle of salt, it was as good a snack as the candy. We kids just assumed that all families snacked on cabbage; we were all adults before we realized that this was not so.

As I pedaled through that sad and dark night in Utah, I reflected back on those times and felt a growing craving to bite into crisp, tangy cabbage. It was a taste reminding me of home and of people who cared about me.

Several days later, I was pedaling through western Colorado. The landscape was unexpected, with the red soil of a plateau and vast fields of onions, peppers, and other vegetables, including cabbage. As I passed one field, a truck pulled out in front of me. The truck was pulling a trailer mounded high with freshly picked green goodness—cabbages!

I smiled to myself, remembering how I'd been craving that taste.

Then, suddenly, a cabbage leaf fluttered from the truck toward me as I pedaled along behind. Then another leaf, and another. As the truck picked up speed, the wind peeled off more and more leaves from the large pale-green rounds. Like manna from Heaven, cabbage leaves floated down around me.

This is incredible! I thought. And so I stopped. Yes, I stopped and picked up a cabbage leaf and went on my way, chewing happily.

You might say it was only a "lucky" coincidence. But I think it was God saying, *You know what? I am still sending down food from Heaven for my people. I know what you're needing, and I'm sending you manna every day.*

I believe He knew exactly what I was craving. My days had been so utterly lonely and desolate; He knew a few fluttering leaves of cabbage would not only taste good to me but would warm my soul. And so He sent cabbage!

Divine dining. We are showered with food sent from Heaven for our hungry souls.

Why would we ignore such special feasts sent from His heart to ours? His Word will speak to our needs as nothing else can. At times, He speaks in other ways, too. He knows exactly what we need. He even uses cabbage leaves.

Look for the divine dining He sends to nourish your soul and give you life on this journey.

38

Angel Food and Trail Magic

In the summer of 2020, as most of this book was being written, people were tired. Just plain tired. A pandemic built barriers between us, and stubborn opinions often pitted neighbor against neighbor, family against family, friend against friend. We grieved the death of life as we used to know it, and many people grieved the death of loved ones. While we tried to deal with and adapt to new realities of COVID life, we witnessed vicious and evil fighting in the streets and the political arena. Some parts of the country lived under the cloud of wildfires, with the scent of smoke always in the air and ash coating sidewalks and cars in a surreal landscape. Others boarded up buildings against nature's hurricanes and the feared tempests of protests. In private, depression, anger, and suicide grew like cancers.

We are tired of trying to deal with it all (it's all still going on, and only God knows what is on the horizon). Most of us desperately need some trail magic in our lives.

One of the greatest delights when I hiked the Appalachian Trail was the unexpected appearance of gifts and help from caring strangers. Sometimes, it was a cooler filled with drinks sitting by the trail in the middle of the woods. No one was around, but the refreshment had been intentionally placed by someone who cared enough about hikers to offer aid along the trail. It could be a person in a parking lot serving sandwiches and calorie-loaded snacks. Trail magic was often food or drink, but it was also a blanket found along the path when you were shivering during unexpectedly cold nights, or the offer of a ride to town when you're walking in a downpour. Trail magic supplied what you needed, when you needed it. It was a sign someone cared about your hike.

The prophet Elijah was in dire need. He was tired. So tired. And discouraged. He'd just had a spectacular triumph against all the pagan priests of the idol Baal, but then he received a death threat. The threat came from the queen, who certainly had the power to carry out whatever she pleased. And what she pleased was to see Elijah dead.

Elijah ran for his life. He tried to put as much distance as possible between him and the avenging queen. For over 100 miles, he traveled south with his servant. Then he went alone on a day's trip into a desert where he finally sat down—exhausted, I imagine—under a shrubby desert tree called a broom tree and had a pity party.

He had done exactly what God had told him to do. Why was this happening to him? Sitting under a tree, he complained to

God. "I've had enough, Lord. I'm done." This life was just too hard. He prayed God would let him die.

I recognize that desert trip, that tree, that lament, that pity party. I recognize the times in the exhausting journey when we say, "I'm done. I've had enough." Are you there right now?

He finally got some sleep but was wakened when a caterer showed up. An angel roused him. Food had been brought to his tree of despair. Elijah saw water and a cake of bread. Angel-food cake.

He ate and drank and laid down and slept again.

In most Bible stories we aren't given all the details, but doesn't it seem odd here that we don't hear Elijah reacting in any way to a stranger in the desert waking him and preparing food for him? He has no questions. His only response seems to be to eat and sleep.

Allow me to project some of our own experiences into this moment with Elijah. Have you had times when you feel dead to what is going on around you? When nothing that happens surprises you, piques your interest, or calls forth any wonder? Even if an angel appeared by your bed one morning to serve you breakfast, would you care? Or would you just pull the covers over your head and go back to sleep? Have you experienced that numbness, that deadness?

The angel came to the broom tree of despair and woke Elijah again. "Get up. Eat. Or else this journey will be too much for you."

Yes, we have all thought the journey was too much for us.

After Elijah had his second meal, he got up and continued his journey. His journey was long, too. After forty days, he arrived at Mount Sinai, the mountain of God. He was still lamenting. Perhaps the reason he came to Sinai was because he wanted to hear from God?

"What are you doing here, Elijah?" asked God. I can imagine that what God was really saying was, "Elijah, I gave you a job to do. So what are you doing here?"

"I did what you asked," replied Elijah. "I've been very zealous serving You. But it's no use. The Israelites will not repent. I'm the only one left who serves you, and they're trying to kill me, too. It's hopeless. It's been a disaster."

I hear my own story.

Paul, what are you doing sitting here lamenting? Get going. Step into the future I have for you.

"But, God, I did what You asked of me. I wrote that book You told me to write. And look what has happened as a result!"

God called Elijah to come out of the cave where he had spent the night to meet Him on the mountainside.

Before Elijah responded, a windstorm tore the mountain apart. I've been battered by a lot of wind.

An earthquake rattled the ground. My earth has been shaken.

A fire roared through. I've felt consumed by fire.

Then God's presence came in a gentle whisper. Elijah heard it. I could not hear the whisper, because I was listening to all the other commotion and tumult in my head.

On one stretch of this journey, I was having trouble hearing that gentle whisper. I could not discern what was the Holy Spirit and what was me. I knew I was standing in my own way, and that God had not moved away from me, but I had moved too far from Him. Maybe I didn't want to admit what I knew. Maybe I didn't know what I knew. Maybe I didn't want to know what I knew. Maybe I didn't even know what I was saying and writing. I know some of you will actually understand this!

When we are hurting, I believe we want to be noticed. We want to be helped. We may say, "Just let me alone," but deep down, we're aching for help. *Someone. Please. Someone with angel food that will give me something that brings strength for this journey. It's all too much for me.*

But where do we find the help we need? A pastor? Counselor? Friend? Where do we go? Who do we open up to?

This journey really is too much for one person to bear, so we need someone else to help us along the way. We need trail magic from caring hearts that understand how exhausting this path is. We need signposts that point us in the right direction. We need to know that someone cares about our journey.

Angels will be sent to help us along the way. God will send manna and angel-food cake in the desert.

It's important to find those people you can open up to. People you trust. People who will be truthful and kind and honor the trust you give them.

The most important person to "open up" to is Jesus Christ. He stands at the door and knocks. He cares more about our journey than anyone else. He can help us more than anyone else. He's our refuge and strength. His promise is to give us full, overflowing life.

He's right there, and all it takes from us is a choice, a decision: *Yes, I will open the door to the Bread of Life.*

Perhaps you are not in any pain right now but you're reading this book because you know someone whose life has been shattered and who is struggling along this journey to healing. You may need to be the caterer who shows up with sustenance for the journey. I truly believe we can make a difference in people's lives. God uses us when we're willing and make ourselves available to Him.

We may not even know the specifics of *who* or *how* we are helping those on this miracle journey. The kind hearts who plan trail magic on the Appalachian Trail often never see the results of their kindness. They don't know who has stopped for a cold drink or who has come along, parched and exhausted, to find candy bars and water. But trail magic, angel-food cake, and signposts all say that *Someone cares about your journey.* What we may think is a small thing to do may provide just that little extra that enables a weary traveler to go one or two more miles.

And to those of you in pain who are traveling along with me on this miracle journey, God uses even us, in all our turmoil and with lives in tatters, to deliver angel food to other weary souls. My hope is that these signposts we're pounding into the ground as we go along will help others who come after us. We all have something, no matter how insignificant it may seem, to offer other weary travelers.

Take a look, fellow traveler, at the ending of Elijah's story in 1 Kings 19. Elijah heard God's gentle whisper. God asked again, *What are you doing here?*

Elijah answered with the same lament of despair and hopelessness.

God replied, "Get going. Step into the future."

GUIDEPOST
↓ ↓ ↓

UNWRAP THE GRAVECLOTHES

39

Out of Your Graves

We've already come a long way on our journey together. Have you noticed that the signposts are coming more quickly? See—the next one is already in sight.

We've tasted divine dining and found it is so good; the call of the cucumbers, leeks, and onions back in Egypt is starting to fade, and we're not looking back quite so often. We're noticing that life is blooming here along our path. Whether we have realized it or not, our graves are breaking open. It's time to unwrap our graveclothes.

Let's revisit Ezekiel 37 and the valley of dry bones. As God and Ezekiel surveyed the devastation, God asked Ezekiel, "Can these bones live again?"

Surely Ezekiel felt the hopelessness in that valley. All logic would say that there was not a breath of possibility there. Zeke neatly sidestepped God's question and said, "You're the only one who knows that answer."

But we can certainly guess what he was thinking, can't we? Because we've been in that dead valley, and we've thought the same thing. *It's hopeless.*

"Prophesy to those bones," God told him. He even gave Ezekiel the words to say: "Dry bones, hear the word of the Lord! This is what the sovereign Lord says to these bones. I will make breath enter you, and you will come to life. I will attach tendons to you and make flesh come upon you and cover you with skin. I will put breath in you, and you will come to life."

So, Ezekiel did as he was told. He had listened carefully and he spoke the words to that valley of devastation. He spoke God's hope over the scene of destruction.

As I read the story, I wondered if the bones had already felt a stirring as God gave His message to Ezekiel? There's an exclamation point after God's instruction to say, "Dry bones, hear the words of the Lord!" There was so much power in those words that I can imagine the bones were already feeling life beginning to flow, even before Ezekiel opened his mouth to repeat the prophecy.

He had not finished prophesying when a noise sounded, a rattling across the valley as bones started to clamber over each other to find their original companions. Without doubt, animals and winged scavengers would have scattered the bones. Can you imagine the noise as all those bones began to move?

Oops, move along. Wrong body.

Where's my missing arm? Oh, here it comes.

Have you seen a right metatarsal that matches this left one?

Yes, the right bones went to the right soldier. Scriptures don't tell us that, but they do tell us that when God restores, He's not haphazard about it. He does it correctly.

As Ezekiel looked on, an amazing medical miracle took place. Across the vast valley, skeletons came together, complete, and lay there, starkly undressed of tendons and skin. Then, as each skeleton was completed, muscles and flesh began to form and cover the lifeless bones.

I would imagine Zeke is speechless by now. Once again, God gives him the words to say. Sure, God could just as easily have commanded breath to enter the resurrected bones, but He instructed Ezekiel to prophesy this: "This is what the Sovereign Lord says, come from the four winds, O breath, and breathe into these slain, that they may live."

Ezekiel spoke as he had been instructed, and breath entered those lifeless bodies. At once, the living dead became fully alive, and as a unit, this vast army rose to their feet.

(I pause to wonder: What must have gone through the minds of these warriors? One second, they were in battle. Some instrument of destruction had found them and inflicted a fatal wound. Their last memories possibly were of loved ones they would never see again. Many years had passed, and the bones, stripped of flesh, became dry and bleached. But now, the soldiers stand there as if they had just been knocked down but have scrambled upright again.

What a potential and-then-what story. And then what happened? Since they were alive, maybe they thought they had won the battle. Undoubtedly, there were also enemy soldiers who had been slain and resurrected. Did they immediately start the battle again? Or perhaps by now they've forgotten all the reasons for battle. Hopefully they marched home, arriving to the bewilderment of their neighbors and families.

Hi, honey, I'm home from the wars!
Who is that man?
Oh, well... you know my mind does wander and wonder.)

God then explained to Ezekiel that those bones were like the exiled nation of Israel who thought all life and hope was gone. Dead. Dried. Lifeless. As far as they could see, their nation was finished.

"But," God said, "tell the people this: 'This is what the Sovereign Lord says...'"

Pay attention! God wants the people to whom He's speaking (and that's us, too) to know that these are the words of the supreme, absolute ruler, the all-mighty, the One who has the final say. This isn't just the hope of a dreamer, the false optimism of some preacher. This is what the Lord God has declared He will do!

God went on: "I am going to open your graves and bring you up from them."

Are you imprisoned in a grave? Are you dream-walking through a dead, lifeless, hopeless existence? Are you standing in the valley after a battle and looking around you, seeing only bleached bones stretching into forever, the aftermath of devastation?

God's message to Israel was clear. He declared His hurting people would once again be brought back to their own land and their lives would be restored.

His message to us is clear. It is the message of the entirety of Scriptures. Hear the word of the LORD: He declares He will bring life, hope, restoration—a future beyond the valley of dried bones. The Creator of all good will not let the enemy have the final say.

Ezekiels

"I will open your graves and bring you out of them. I will bring you back to your land where you can live again."

Wow! Talk about happening upon a cool spring of water in a dry desert! Life restored! This sounds so refreshing. It's what we long for.

But oh, it seems so impossible when we've been destroyed by loss, a disaster, a trust broken, a death, a betrayal. We're dead emotionally, mentally, physically, spiritually.

The first step in God's plan to bring that army back to life was to bring the bones together. They came together, but they were still dead. They needed breath.

God created man by breathing His own breath into dust. He could have simply waved His hand and blown life into those dead bodies. But He brought Ezekiel into the plan and the process; He had Ezekiel speak God's prophetic words over the valley.

People who have gone through devastation need an Ezekiel to intercede for them. They need an Ezekiel to speak God's hope over them. Do you have Ezekiels in your life?

Ezekiels are not the ones who bring life to dead bones, but they point us to the one Person who can give us life and hope. We need those Ezekiels. We need to be led to Jesus. Perhaps you need to meet Him for the first time. Or perhaps you just need to be gently turned in the right direction to get back to Him.

In many stretches of this journey, we feel so alone. There were times I felt that I was walking this hard, hard path all by myself, and I felt no one else understood and no one had answers or help for me.

At the time of our breakup, She suggested I talk to a counselor. *No, I don't need that,* I thought. *I've got God. I'm strong. I don't need a counselor. I know why I'm hurting.*

What I didn't know, though, was how to get out of the hurt. And when the pain is so horrible, you have to have help.

Whether or not you seek the aid of a counselor during your journey will be your decision. But I am here to tell you that God enlists Ezekiels of all walks of life to prophesy breath and life and hope to us. Ezekiels help us come up out of our graves.

During a time I was hurting badly from the breakup and I was struggling with getting answers to my questions, a package came in the mail. A lady I had never met sent me a journal that she had written while reading *Hiking Through.* While she was reading the book, she thought of sending her notes to me, but she never did so. Until, a year later, she felt the Holy Spirit say, *Do it now.* She included a note with the journal, saying it would be "a miracle if this gets to you" and it "makes no logical sense at all" for her to send it, but she was being obedient to the Spirit's prompting.

I was struggling with so many questions and emotions, and many of the things she had written—even things she quoted that I myself had written years ago—encouraged me. I was amazed. She had felt the Holy Spirit say, *Do it,* and she did it, even though she couldn't understand the reason. His timing was exactly right. Her obedience brought Ezekiel prophecies into my life.

Even more encouraging than what she or I had written, I felt a trembling of hope and life within me because I knew God had spoken to her, asking her to speak to me. God knew how dead I was. He had called an Ezekiel to prophecy breath into my dead bones.

Other people spoke into my life—once I had opened myself to help. Many times we're reluctant to admit we need help; we're uncomfortable with laying out our messes in front of others' eyes. But it is important that we let others help us. Talk. Don't be so independent. I don't care how strong you are, going through a deep loss takes so much out of you. I know. I barely recognized myself at times. This is a hard journey.

I believe that God sends Ezekiels even when we aren't seeing or hearing them because we're buried so deep in our graves of pain. But God is all about breaking open our graves. He won't give us up as dead.

In John 11, we have the account of Jesus visiting the grave of Lazarus, His dear friend. Lazarus was buried in a cave, and Jesus opened that grave and called Lazarus back to life. The dead man—now living—came out of the cave. The graveclothes were still wrapped around him, binding him.

"Unwrap him and let him go!" Jesus told several mourners standing at the gravesite. Apparently, Lazarus was wrapped tightly enough that he couldn't shake off the trappings of the grave himself. Someone had to unwrap him.

I was wrapped very tightly in my pain. I needed help getting those graveclothes off. I'd been grappling with so much for so long. But I did want to change. I started reaching out to several people, and I felt like Lazarus being unwrapped.

I don't care what it is in life that you're wrestling with, two things are necessary: You have to want to change, and you need the help of others.

Help came from people in all situations of life and in so many ways—it's not always in words written or spoken.

Months after God had told me to get going and step into the future, I was still having sleepless nights. One night was particularly horrible. Five hours of tossing, turning, thoughts going round and round and round, the pain of the breakup still burning in me.

"God," I finally said in the morning, "I'm just so tired of endings." The pain of loss, death, breakups—I was tired of it all.

God said, *Everything is going to end—except my love. That will never end.*

That evening, I met with a local businessman who was hoping to hike the Appalachian Trail for a week. He had asked me for information, and I agreed to meet. Instead of coffee at a local restaurant, he requested that I join him at the top of a hill where he keeps his two-person hang glider. I drove up through a field and found the place. He was already there.

"Do you want to go up?" he asked.

Well, I thought, *I'm ready to die.* So I agreed. He strapped me in, and we took off.

The evening was beautiful. We glided over my town and swooped above cornfields. Geese went flying. The sun was setting.

I had headphones, and my pilot turned on music. "How Great Thou Art" sounded in my ears as I took in God's creation from a new viewpoint. Unexpectedly, I felt peace settling over me.

We made a turn to fly over my neighborhood, and another song began: "The Love of God."

My favorite song.

As we came in for a landing, the favorite verse of my favorite song began:

> Could we with ink the oceans fill,
> And were the skies of parchment made,
> Were every stalk on earth a quill,
> And every man a scribe by trade;
> To write the love of God above
> Would drain the oceans dry;
> Nor could the scroll contain the whole
> Though stretched from sky to sky.

That verse was supposedly written by an insane man. The words were found scrawled on the walls of a prison cell where he was held, and they were preserved by a priest. Hundreds of years later, when Frederick M. Lehman—who had also suffered huge losses—was writing a song about the love of God, he remembered that someone had given him these words. They fit so well with what he had already written that he added them as the third stanza to his song.

Another one hundred years later, I was up there in the sky, singing the song with heart and voice.

God's love will not end! I can count on that.

After the rough week, I could feel the graveclothes unwrapping.

Back home, I sent my Ezekiel a text: *You blessed me tonight.*

Are You? Will You?

As the Israelites traveled through the desert toward the land God had promised them, they were often met with hostility. I would imagine this massive influx of people was quite unwelcome to those already living in the land. The travelers were also targets of marauders. Traveling in family groups, they could not have looked like an organized, equipped army but more like vulnerable prey.

So the attacks came.

Can you identify with this? We're traveling along this journey, looking forward to a land God has promised us—but often set upon by adversaries determined to keep us from claiming a good land.

It can be such a difficult road.

We're often attacked by the enemy who wants to block our path. The one who wants to defeat God's plans would rather we abandon this journey. He would like nothing more than for us to give up when we are so tired. He'd love for us to believe his whispered lies that the land of restoration and renewed life is only a dream, a place we'll never find.

How many times the Israelites gave in to this thinking! They longed to go back to Egypt—to slavery! They grumbled. They even tried to organize revolts against Moses' leadership. And they ended up living in the desert for 40 years—and dying there.

We who travel together on this miracle journey cannot let each other fall along the way.

Exodus 17 gives us an account of one attack against the desert wanderers. The Amalekites attacked. Young Joshua was already a rising leader, and he organized those who would fight. Moses knew the secret to victory, though, and he took Aaron and Hur to the top of a hill overlooking the battle. There, Moses held high the staff of God, that staff that God had used to perform miracles in the rescue of the Israelites in Egypt.

Now, the staff was key in winning the battle against attack. As long as Moses held up the staff, the Israelites dominated the combat. But as the day went on, Moses' arms began to tire. His muscles quivered with the strain; his arms slowly began to fall lower and lower. Maybe he even took a short break, just to rest for a moment. We aren't told that in the Scripture account, but we are told that whenever he lowered his arms, the enemy prevailed.

So Aaron and Hur found a rock for Moses to sit on. That might have helped his legs, but his arms continued to weaken. Finally, Aaron stood on one side of Moses and Hur on the other, and they held up the trembling arms, keeping that staff raised high and steady over the skirmish in the valley below. This went on until sunset, and the Israelites won the battle.

When we are in the deepest pain, we see ourselves in Moses. We cannot keep going. We're exhausted. We have nothing more in us. We need help just to survive.

But there are many times God calls upon us to be Aaron or Hur. We are still on the journey ourselves, but others traveling with us need us to steady them and hold them up.

I was suffering, and Ezekiels came along to breathe words of life over me. Then I discovered they were plodding along on their own journey, themselves struggling from signpost to signpost, from strength to strength. This caught me off guard. It amazed me, actually. So many of the people who have spoken into my life during this journey have also been fighting battles along their own road to restoration.

We need help in this journey, but God has designed the miracle journey with the intention that we are also going to help others along the way. God moved other people who were struggling as much as I was to help me. He asks me to do the same. He asks you to do the same.

I want to help other people. I've prayed God will use me to touch other lives. On my knees in that prayer, I heard God's answer: *I will help you, but you are going to feel others' pain.*

As trembling arms start falling, who better to hold them up than arms that know exactly what that exhaustion feels like? Who better to help others along this rugged path than those who have also struggled with its challenges?

What has God planned for you, even as you groan in your grave?

Will you be standing by some of these signposts in the desert, encouraging other weary travelers?

Will He send you as His angel to take by the hand someone whose life is burning behind them and who is paralyzed in one place?

Has He given you words to prophecy life and breath to bones of dead dreams and wounded faith?

Will you be the chef He asks to cater a meal of divine dining to an exhausted traveler?

Are you witnessing Jesus breaking open a grave, and do you hear His command to unwrap their graveclothes?

Jesus had to be a human being like us, He had to suffer in the same ways we do, so that He could, in the end, be the One and Only who could save us and is saving us. He had to go through it all so He could help us.

Like forging strong metal in the fire, God forges us to be His ministers to others going through similar pain. We are *meant* to be a place of springs in the desert, offering living water. We are *meant* to be Jesus' partners in other people's miracle journeys.

We may think we don't have it in us. We are only now crawling out of our own graves. We've been devastated. Like the dead bones, we were destroyed. We have nothing to give.

That's exactly when God can use us. In our weakness, He is strongest. If we think we are strong and complete, we leave little room for Him to work. We think we've "got it."

It seems to go against all logic, but He can use our brokenness in amazing ways. He asks only that we are open to His Spirit and are willing.

Will we accept the mission?

If You Can Use Any of This…

I am farther along in the wilderness journey than I was a few months ago. I'm not quite to the land of restoration yet, but I'm getting there. Hope keeps me going. I now have faith that I'll soon be at the next signpost and there will be someone there to prophecy breath into me and that breath will take me to the next place of strength…

Here's a collection of random thoughts that may help unwrap your graveclothes. I offer them to those of you who have experienced the devastation of a romantic breakup or divorce.

These are for you who have had relationships betrayed and broken. Your life may have been shattered in other ways, and none of the following may apply to you—you may even find these thoughts incomprehensible to you in your situation. If so, feel free to skip forward to the next chapter, which is applicable to everyone who has seen any kind of trouble. This chapter is specifically for situations like my breakup.

I've had many helps along the course of this journey. At one point, I was reading two books, both with broken hearts on the cover. One was written by a woman who took a gentle approach to dealing with hurt and the pursuit of healing. Reading her perspective on breakups and broken hearts was like being touched with a feather.

The author of the other book was a man who sounded just like me. As I perused the pages of his book, I read statements I myself had already written or spoken in almost the same vocabulary and tone! He expressed feelings of pain and betrayal that were exactly what I was feeling. The details of his breakup were so similar to mine that reading the book was sometimes an eerie experience. It was published the same month and year of my breakup.

Reading this second book was brutal. He was speaking directly to me. He pounded nails of truth into me—truths that I had been trying to deny or at least ignore. I needed the gentle touch of the first writer, but I also needed to hear and accept the truths presented so bluntly and forcibly in the second book.

From those books, conversations with people who came into my life in God's timing, and my own insights, here are fragments of my thinking and feeling. They are raw and in no particular order. Take what is helpful to you, leave the rest. I have a feeling that as I push forward in the journey, I may throw out some of these myself. Or maybe modify them. But sorting through all of this is part of the wilderness experience, a necessary exercise in our journey to healing.

Self-esteem

Rejection is horrible. It makes you feel worthless. It's humiliating to realize you're not as special as you thought you were. Seeing how easily you can be replaced by another destroys your spirit. Rejection whispers—no, it *shouts*—that you weren't good enough, you weren't enough.

But be kind to yourself. You need to like yourself, even love yourself. I know that's difficult for some of us. But you are headed toward healing when you realize you *are* good enough. What the other person has done to you does not define your worth, especially your worth in God's eyes. The truth is, we are special. We are sons and daughters of Almighty God. What someone has done to you says more about who they are than who you are. You deserve better. Find someone who is worthy of your love.

Brutal Truths

Don't expect the person who hurt you to be the one to help you heal. They probably can't help you and almost certainly do not want to.

They left you because they wanted to. They lied to you because they wanted to. They betrayed you because they chose to.

The lady author with the gentle feather wrote, "Reject the rejecter." That seems harsh to me. Yet I realized that I never truly released my former love. I never let her go. At the same time, I would admit that I didn't really want to keep what I was hanging onto. How does one let go? But then, why wouldn't you want to let go?

The truth is, that person who left you, deceived you, lied to you, or abandoned you was looking out for themselves and didn't care about you.

Trust is an amazing gift we give to someone else. I gave someone my trust and believed she would take care of it. Instead, trust was destroyed. Realize that every person chooses how they are going to treat the gift they're given. That person who betrayed your trust made a choice.

Questions

I realized, finally, that it has to be okay that I don't have answers. Not everything in life is going to make sense. This was difficult for me because my mind demands that I can arrange and file my thoughts logically, but that is never going to happen with the situation around the breakup. I won't have answers. I'm getting to the place where I don't need them. Actually, more than answers from her, I am now desiring to know what God wants of me.

Replace *Why* questions with *How can I learn from this?* Even if we're given answers to the *Why?*, the answers will probably never satisfy us.

If you're ending a relationship

Some relationships need to end. Try to end them honorably. We're human, I know, and we often don't realize how our actions affect others. It took me years to see what I had done to some people when I *thought* I was acting rationally. I only understood how much I had hurt others when someone else hurt me.

This is a plea to those who are ending a relationship: be genuine, honest, and honorable.

If you lie or deceive one person in order to start a relationship with someone else, then that new relationship has been founded on deception. And it means the "other person" you've found is someone who is okay with deception. Relationships that start with deception probably aren't going to work out too well—after all, both parties have already accepted it as a means to an end.

Aloneness

Whether by death, divorce, or breakup, the person you counted on to be there is no longer there and will never be there again. For a long time, you will feel incomplete. Do not look for someone just to fill that empty space. We truly have to find joy alone before we're ready for another relationship.

I don't want to be alone. You don't want to be alone. I'm feeling the pain of aloneness. But we really do need to be okay with aloneness. Look inward, see who you really are. Find new hobbies, new interests, make friends. Revive the dreams you once had—before the romantic disaster.

I don't want a "replacement." I want someone sent by God. Someone I can love.

When you realize that what you're looking back to in the past was never as good as what you will have in the future… then you know you've made progress in the miracle journey.

Speaking truth

If there is a new relationship for you, be totally honest with that person. I hate lies. If a person's going to lie to me, I cannot trust them. I am worth more than that. Aren't you worth more than being lied to? If someone has deceived you, they don't deserve you or your trust.

Yet I know that in past relationships I did withhold truth when I should have spoken. Now, I strive to be totally honest. I tell people what they mean to me. It's so much easier.

Your peace and victory

At the end of the day, you are in control of your own stress level, peace, and happiness. Do not give to another person the ability to control and determine your peace and well-being.

Don't hold grudges. What's most important is how you maintain your own peace of mind. Grudges have no effect on the focus of your anger, but they take a huge toll on you. People don't always act with good intentions, and yes, people aren't always genuine, but that's on them.

Stop seeing yourself as a victim. Be a victor.

Good Proclamations

On the glider one morning, I was taken to Psalm 37. It's a song that has several well-known and oft-quoted verses.

The psalm opens by telling us not to fret because of evil people. They will soon wither like the grass. The people that hurt you will fade away. Instead of thinking so much and stewing about them, "trust in the Lord and do good; dwell in the land and enjoy safe pasture" (verse 3).

That's quite a shift of focus, isn't it? We consciously pivot from thinking about the ones who've hurt and wronged us to delighting in the "land" where God has brought us.

That "good land" can be everything from the physical, real environment and the beauty of natural settings to the good gifts He has given to us. Those gifts include our salvation, His presence with us, His healing in our lives, our families, the everyday joys, the blessings of friendship—the list could go on and on.

We are not to simply exist one day to the next. The command to "dwell in the land" implies purposeful living and thinking in the life He makes possible.

Verse 4 really spoke to me. I imagine many folks have grasped this verse when they longed for something with all their heart: "Delight yourself in the Lord and he will give you the desires of your heart."

I would guess that many of us read that verse and focus on the last clause—the promise that we will be given the desires of our hearts. Part of my brain joked with God: "I wouldn't have to have *every* desire of my heart; just a few would be nice." But the words that really came alive to me that morning were the first five, the ones most of us have not explored or experienced in any depth: *Delight yourself in the Lord.*

Sitting there on the back porch, I looked up. One small white cloud drifted slowly through an intensely blue sky.

"God, I delight in You this morning," I said.

I got up and walked around the driveway. Noticing a bird in the tree, I repeated, "Delight yourself in the Lord."

My jasmine plant finally had one blossom. *Delight yourself in the Lord.*

I love flowers and took photos of more of the blooms in my flower beds. The honeysuckle had just started showing its colors, and there was another new, perfect burst of pure yellow on the hibiscus plant that just keeps producing joy after joy this year. *Delight yourself in the Lord.*

The sun was coming up, but wisps of morning fog still hung in the air. I love fog. It's just amazing. *I delight in You, Lord.*

This is a good exercise for each day of our restoration journey. Set a routine time during which you open your eyes to what is around you. Look closely at your natural setting. The beauty is there. Repeat your delight in the land He has given you. *Delight in Him.*

Then survey the landscape of your life. Your delight might be in many other things besides His creation: His Word, His Spirit, the people He has placed in your life, the obvious ways in which He has worked this week in a situation, the thing or person He brought into your life just when you needed it. Delight in Him. James says every good gift is from the Father. Enjoy the good gifts He has given you and everything He's done for you.

Hiking the Appalachian Trail, I was often so busy looking down at the ground, watching for rocks and roots and other possible trouble in the path ahead, that I sometimes had to tell myself, "Just stop and look around." Then I'd see the details and the beauty.

What brings you joy? Maybe rocking a drowsy baby to sleep. Gooey chocolate cake, and ice cream, of course. The first taste of coffee in the morning. Knowing someone loves you. The joy of watching your children being parents. Making a memory with grandchildren. Just "being" with your siblings. Coconut cake!

As we go through our wilderness experience, lamenting our losses, there are times we just need to stop, look around, and most importantly, look up. That's where our redemption lies—in God's arm, reached out to us. Thank Him. Thank Him for what He has done. Take a good look at what He's doing for you now. Thank Him for Ezekiels. For good gifts in the midst of a pandemic. This is not just striving to find a silver lining. It's looking for God's hand at work, knowing that He is the Lord, and that He will always be the Great Shepherd of your soul. There is no better way to shift our focus from our misery and the wrongs that have been done to us, to the good land He has given us.

Lazarus needed the help of others to unwrap his graveclothes. We need others, too, but there are also ways we can loosen our own garments of the grave. This practice of delighting in our Lord will help us do so.

He is planning to give you the desires of your heart; but first, you have to take delight in Him, which means trusting Him and committing everything to Him. Take a moment to think about what all is included in that *everything*—the joys and the sorrows, the dreams and the disappointments, the energy and the weakness, the loved ones and the enemies, *everything*. Trust Him in everything. Commit everything to Him.

A few days after that morning, I was out on our walking trail and praying for some of the people who have come to walk with me on this journey, people God has sent into my life recently. My former love came to mind. I was able to pray that God would give her the desires of her heart. I actually said it aloud. I think I am beginning to mean it.

I confess I've had moments when I did not delight in God. There was one day in particular that I was walking on our local trail and dialoguing with Him, but my frustration boiled over. I yelled at Him.

"Can I trust You?" I shouted.

Ezekiel 37 contains more messages for us. Verse 13 says, "Then you, my people, will know that I am the LORD, when I open your graves and bring you up from them." Four times in the chapter, God repeats that what He does will cause His people to know that He is God, He is Sovereign, and He does what He promises.

When Lazarus died, Jesus said that everything that had happened was for the glory of God and so that people would believe in Him. I've said this: "If God can fix me and heal me, He deserves the glory."

As Ezekiels prophesy breath to us and others help to unwrap our graveclothes, let's open our eyes to see that it is God working, God restoring, God redeeming. The miracle journey is His idea. He will not leave us in the grave. His unfailing love is guiding us home. Delight in that. And give Him all the glory as the graveclothes fall away.

Great are the works of the LORD;
they are pondered by all who delight in them.
Psalm 111:2

It is good to proclaim your unfailing love in the morning,
and your faithfulness in the evening.
Psalm 92:2 NLT

GUIDEPOST
↓ ↓ ↓

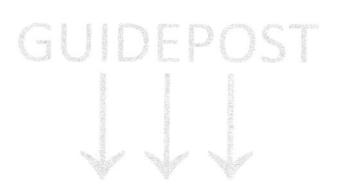

HIS ARM IS NOT TOO SHORT

44

How Long is God's Arm?

How long is God's arm?

How would your faith answer that question?

Let's look at biblical accounts, one from Numbers 11, the second from Jeremiah 32.

The great multitude traveling through the desert were getting sick of manna. Every day, the same menu. They had lost their awe of the miracle from Heaven. They looked back at the variety of things they'd eaten in Egypt, and they especially craved meat. In tent after tent, people were whining and complaining about eating manna every day, and "the anger of the LORD was kindled greatly."

Moses was upset, too, and he vented his frustration to God. "Why did you give me this job? It's too much for me to handle alone. Why did you give me this burden? Why not kill me instead?"

The Lord gave Moses some relief—He chose 70 men to help carry the load of leadership.

And this was God's message for Moses to give to the people: "You want meat? You will have it—until it comes out your nostrils and makes you sick."

God wasn't angry with the people because they were hungry for meat. He was angry because they had rejected Him, complained about His rescue of them from slavery, and scorned the blessing of food He sent every day.

Moses was still overwhelmed. "How in the world are we going to feed them? How am I supposed to find meat for all of them? Even if we butchered all our flocks and herds, we wouldn't have enough."

And God answered, "Is my arm too short? You will see whether or not I can do what I say I will do."

The quail came in on a wind from the sea and literally flooded the camp and the area for miles around.

Hundreds of years later, the prophet Jeremiah was thrown in jail in Judah because he was preaching such a disturbing message: "Babylon will soon destroy Jerusalem because our people have refused to obey God." They had turned their backs on the God who had saved them from Egypt and were worshipping other gods.

But along with this prophetic message of God's discipline, Jeremiah received strange instructions. He was to buy a field from his cousin. Buy property? When Babylon was going to capture and destroy everything? When their city and country were going to be devastated and many of the people be scattered in exile?

Jeremiah bought the property, went through all the official procedures, and stored the deed safely away. Why? Because the Lord had also promised that the people of Judah would be brought back. There was hope of restoration, and Jeremiah believed God would do exactly as He said He would do.

In his prayer, Jeremiah recounts all the things God has done: "Ah, Sovereign LORD, you have made the heavens and the earth by your great power and outstretched arm. You brought your people out of Egypt by a strong hand and an outstretched arm." He looked back at their history, and he believed God could keep His promise that even though the country would be devastated, there would be restoration.

And we hear God's response: "I am God of all peoples of the world. Is anything too hard for me?"

Nearly every reader can identify with dead bones—death of hope, death of trust, death of love, death of family, lost job, life shattered by tragedy. I doubt that you would have stayed with me this long if you have not suffered something like this. You may have felt abandoned by God or punished by God. You know what it is to walk through the valley of such deaths.

But now, as we near the Jordan River and look forward to settling in the Land of Promise, as you look back at the long journey we've traveled together, consider how long God's arm is.

Has He not brought you out of the disaster that was Egypt or the hard sojourn of discipline in Babylon? Is He not guiding you on this path to the land He promised you? Is He not bringing you back to where He wants you to live and flourish in peace and joy? Has He not given you miraculous food from Heaven, made streams in your desert, and provided angels and prophets to speak hope into your journey?

Has He not made a way for you through this wilderness? And has He not given us each other to travel together and help one another?

Don't you feel His breath stirring your dead bones as He calls flesh back to life and speaks hope into you once again?

His words to Ezekiel and the people were, "Then you'll know that I am the Lord." His words to us are, "Know that I am the Lord. Know that my arm is long enough."

Can we trust Him to give us what we need the most? His arm is long enough to do that.

Can He bring us comfort and joy instead of sorrow? His arm is long enough.

Can He turn our wasteland into well-watered gardens filled with bounty? His arm is long enough.

One more account of God's provision.

Abraham finally had the son he'd been promised. Isaac was going to fulfill all the promises God had made to Abraham. Through him, all the nations of the world would be blessed.

Then God asked Abraham to give up his son. The father was to sacrifice his son on an altar on a mountain God would show him.

What do you suppose Abraham thought? Did he agonize over this command from God? How could God require such a thing? Did Abraham question, argue, lie awake at night pleading with God?

We don't know. But we do know that Abraham believed God would keep all His promises. He believed so firmly and completely that Scriptures call him the father of all who have faith. We do know that Abraham believed God could even bring his son back to life (Hebrews 11:19).

When what is happening to us just doesn't seem to make sense, do we believe just as firmly and unshakably in God's promises?

We have clues about Abraham's faith. When they finally reached the mountain, Abraham told the servant who was traveling with them to wait below the mountain. "We will go and sacrifice, then we will come back to you." He's fully expecting Isaac to return with him.

Isaac probably had his own questions about this strange trip, and he finally asked: "Father, we've brought the wood and the fire, but where is the lamb for the sacrifice?"

Abraham's answer of faith: "God will provide the sacrifice."

At this point, I weep. You see what this scene is pointing toward? Or rather, *who* this scene points toward? God is showing us what He will do for us.

The sacrifice for me: Jesus.

God provided the sacrifice. God gave up His own Son to provide a way for the world to come back to Him. To provide a way for *me* to become a part of His family. In His Son, all the nations of the world are blessed. His Son fulfills all the promises He has made.

Before Abraham's knife plunged into Isaac, bound on the altar, an angel stopped him. Abraham then saw a ram, caught in the bushes nearby. A ram for the sacrifice. God had provided.

Abraham called the place "The Lord will provide."

Can we look back at times that we completely trusted God and He provided? If so, we can look toward the future and know with confidence that God will provide. We can believe that He can and will do what He says He will do.

His arm is not too short. He can do it.

45

Bones Can Get to the Promised Land

The book of Psalms is filled with praise and hope and lament. One of the laments that often comes is "Oh, Lord, how long do I need to wait? How long must this go on?"

Even David, that man "after God's own heart," struggled with that question.

We have struggled with it, too. The words may have come out, strangled by our sobs, or they may have been screamed at God in frustration. God knows all about our frustration. He knows how tired we become on this journey.

We can be confident, though, that even when we feel this journey will never end, or if the path ahead is very foggy, or if our destination seems uncertain, *there is a Canaan ahead*.

Right now, we can start thanking God for the destination.

Joseph's bones inspire me to have confidence in God. Dead bones can get to the Promised Land.

Joseph spent all of his adult life in Egypt, yet somehow he held onto his faith in God and God's promises. He knew all about what God had promised his great-grandfather concerning a land his people could call their own. He died in Egypt, after his family had been settled there for many decades. Yet he believed God would keep His promise.

He believed it so firmly that he gave these instructions:

> "Soon I will die," Joseph told his brothers, "but God will surely come to help you and lead you back out of this land of Egypt. He will bring you back to the land he solemnly promised to give to Abraham, to Isaac, and to Jacob." Then Joseph made the sons of Israel swear an oath, and he said, "When God comes to help you and lead you back, you must take my bones with you." (Genesis 50:24, 25)

Do you hear the confidence Joseph had in God's long arm? "God *will surely come* to help you." "*When* [not *if*] God comes to help..." Even when there was no visible sign that the family of Jacob would ever get back to their own country, Joseph was sure it would happen. God had promised it.

Almost 300 years went by, and Joseph's family was still living in a foreign land. Finally, God spoke to Moses and said, "It's time to get my people out of Egypt."

There is no way I wanted to wait 400 years for God to help me. How about you?

Apparently, Joseph's request and the oath that was taken were remembered and passed from one generation to the next because when Moses led the exodus, Joseph's bones were carried along with them. We aren't told much about the journey the bones had to endure, but I do wonder about one thing: Sometimes when Moses was especially weary and frustrated, did he sit down and have a one-way conversation with those bones? Joseph would surely have understood all Moses was going through.

The bones made it to the Promised Land. They were buried in the field Joseph's father had given him over 400 years before. The bones settled in the same area of Samaria where Jacob's well is located—the well where Jesus met the Samaritan woman and revealed to her that He was the hoped-for Messiah.

Joseph had great confidence in God. Even though the circumstances of his life made God's promise look impossible, he believed God. Confidently, patiently, he believed what God had said.

Do we have such firm confidence in our God? Can we say unequivocally that God *will* bring us through this journey to restoration? Not *if. Will.*

For the days when our confidence flags, we have a psalm that answers the psalms of lament. Psalm 27, a song of encouragement and confidence, has lines that we can all place *upon* our hearts.

The Lord is my light and my salvation—so why should I be afraid? If we are depending on the God of all nations, the God whose arm is powerful enough to do anything, the God who has claimed us as His own and has died so that we can live, the God who has given us His Spirit, why should we feel weak and afraid on this journey? *Even if a mighty army comes against me and if I am attacked, I will remain confident.*

Teach me how to live, O Lord. Lead me along the right path. This is a prayer for every day. Then we can walk in confidence. We know He walks with us, beside us, ahead of us, behind us. He'll teach us the best way to live. We can pray this and believe it because He has said He will do it.

Even though my enemies are constantly threatening, yet I am confident I will see the Lord's goodness while I am here in the land of the living. Psalm 27 is confidence in the midst of trouble. It is the assurance of Psalm 23:5, that even when surrounded by enemies, we are still receiving a feast of good things from our God. He is so good to us. Look back over our journey. We've seen His goodness, haven't we?

Wait patiently for the Lord. Be brave and courageous. Yes, wait patiently for the Lord. But surely not 400 years, Lord? Please, no! That admonition to wait is repeated. I guess we need to hear it again and again. Because waiting patiently is not something that's easy.

Yet it is the patient waiting that sees the Lord's goodness even while we are still trudging through the desert. Those who wait patiently and learn from Him how to live will be brave and courageous. And they will see the Promised Land.

A New Thing

I'm close.

We're close.

The Jordan River is up ahead. The land of promised restoration is just beyond. Or, if you've likened your journey to the Babylonian exile, then you've packed up your seventy years of life and are now headed back home to the life God promised you. Whichever way you see this journey after devastation and loss, we are headed back home.

We've spent a good deal of time with the ancient prophets. They have so much to say about wandering, disobedience, and God's discipline, but their writings abound with promise of restoration.

Isaiah 43 shines with hope and comfort. It presents the words of the Lord who has created us and redeemed us. He tells us not to be afraid, no matter what we have to walk through. We are precious and loved by Him, and no one can tear us out of His hand. Verse 19 is for us, right now, in our journey to restoration:

> "See, I am doing a new thing! Now it springs up; do you not perceive it? I am making a way in the wilderness and streams in the wasteland."

He is doing new things in my life and your life. He is making a way for us through this wilderness. Can we see the new things He is doing?

I admit, sometimes the view is very foggy. My sights are clouded by discouragement, loneliness, regrets, views in the wrong direction (yes, still occasionally looking back), the pain of betrayal, the loss of love, the lack of answers.

But I want that fog to disperse. I want a clearer vision. I want to see and know whatever "new" God is doing!

We've used numerous metaphors throughout the book. Let's just take a quick review.

We are like that house Marv and I tore apart and renovated. Some things have to go to make place for the new. The old often puts up strong resistance; transformation comes through pain. God is the architect in this process. He has plans for a new that outshines the old. The Holy Spirit is the workman knocking down old walls, building a new according to the Architect's plans.

We've considered what it means to take up our cross, for the old us to die daily and be resurrected to a new life.

We've watched Lazarus come shuffling out of his cave grave and heard Jesus' command to unwrap the graveclothes. Can you imagine the and-then-what story of Lazarus and his sisters after that day? A man came out of the grave to live again. And then what? What must his life after the grave have been like? We're unwrapping our graveclothes. We're being given new life. What might await us in the days ahead?

We've walked through the valley of dead bones, surveyed crushed hopes and dreams, wondered if they can ever live again. Not only can they be given shape and flesh and breath once again, they can get to the Promised Land! Perhaps your dead bones are feeling the life stirring; maybe they're even ready to get up and run to Canaan!

We've learned to know Joseph even better. We felt his despair as his brothers seized him and threw him into a pit. What do you imagine he thought when he was pulled out again only to realize he was being sold as a slave? He could never have guessed then what God had planned for him in the coming years. And it was years—he had a long, hard journey before he saw clearly how God had worked His plan.

Probably one of the most beautiful and amazing examples God has given us of the miraculous new things He can do happens constantly in the cycles of nature—when a monarch butterfly miraculously breaks through the restriction of its chrysalis and emerges in its magnificent new splendor. Within that tight confinement, a miracle journey has been going on. A worm has transformed into a monarch.

Where are you now in your chrysalis time? Still wrapped tightly? Still feeling the stress of pain that binds you? Or are you beginning to sense the magnificent new about to emerge? Perhaps you have already broken through what was holding you so tightly, and you have spread your wings to dry and gain their strength in the light of the Son. Perhaps you're ready to flutter over the Jordan into your promised land.

Each of us has our own story. The specifics of our loss and devastation vary. We've all known pain, despair, loneliness, discouragement, and questioning. We've struggled with anger (both righteous and vengeful), a wounded self-worth, and doubting God. But God *is* doing something new in each of our lives. He has been working His miracle even when it seemed we were pulled out of a pit only to be sold into slavery.

For a while, all I could think of was how She had robbed me of nearly four years of my life. Or, put another way, how I had wasted that many years. As I look back now, I can say that God didn't waste those four years. He was working on me.

I have learned how deeply I can love. It was love that brought such pain into my life, but I know now the love that is possible for me. I believe everything I've gone through and what I've learned has prepared me to be an amazing husband. (I like to think that, anyway.) A year ago, I was too low to even think of anything good coming from this season of my life.

God has shifted my perspective to an eternal view. For a long time, I wanted an explanation from Her, but I'm close to the point where I no longer need it.

Now I'm grappling more with the question: Did I fail to honor God? Did I fail His plan? From the very start of our relationship, we thought it was a gift from God. Then what happened? My focus at first was on how She had broken my trust. But now I'm troubled with the thought that I broke God's trust. Was His plan for us to write that book together? How many people might have been helped by such a book? If that was God's plan, we failed. I spent so much time thinking about what She did to me, but now I'm seeing what I did to Her—I did not pursue what we should have been pursuing.

There are days when a reminder of the past pops up. Then I still look back. But more and more, I am asking God, *What are You getting me ready for?*

I'm learning to see God's discipline as His kindness and love for me.

What have you learned?

What miracle has been happening in your life during this journey?

Let's not miss what He has been and is doing. He's making a way for us through this wilderness, He's guiding us along the path, and we're almost there. And we're soon going to find that He's even gone ahead of us, making a way into our future.

The Seasons of Life

Summer is over
Peaceful days, starry nights
Sunbeams and rainbows
Autumn arrives
Vibrantly colored leaves
Gentle breezes
Warm blankets and campfires
Then... the long winter
Cold and lonely evenings
Dreary days
Storms on the horizon
Will it ever end?
But spring breaks through
Promises of life again
Cleansing rain
Life anew
Give us this reminder, Lord,
Through the seasons of life
If summer can't endure
Help us through the cold and lonely
Storms of winter
Though we're dormant, grow our roots
Give us strength to look ahead
To see new life start to bloom
With hope for another summer

-- Susan Kocak

GUIDEPOST
↓ ↓ ↓

GO TAKE THE LAND!

The Story in the Scars

I have a scar on my right hand. It happened several years ago while I was pressure washing my house. It was a powerful pressure washer, and I was trying to be very cautions with the wand, since a blast from the wand to one's skin could do serious damage.

I was wearing leather gloves to protect my hands. Suddenly the wand slipped out of my grasp, and as I reached for it, a laser of high-pressure water shot beneath my right glove. A sizable chunk of flesh was blown from my hand.

It was so painful and so bloody.

Over the next few days, a scab formed; and after a few weeks, the scab vanished but left a ragged scar.

I can now look at that scar and recall precisely the time and place of that mishap.

You see, the story is in the scar.

I was a young boy. My cousin and I were in the woods where a small creek flowed. We were dam builders that day. We stacked rocks across the flow, creating a small reservoir. Then we began skipping stones across the surface. We picked up larger and larger stones until we were skipping rocks. With the correct angle of the toss, the right velocity of the throw, and the right geometry of the rock, any rock will skip. One rock about twelve inches in size slid gracefully across our little dam.

But on one return trip, the rock unceremoniously hit my right shin. It was one of the most painful mishaps of my young life, and it left a gouge in my shin that bled profusely.

This wound was reluctant to heal. It became infected, and the wound festered for weeks. At last, a scab formed and eventually it, too, vanished—leaving only a scar. Whenever I see that scar on my right shin, I'm taken back to a place in time when two young boys dammed a creek.

You see, the story is in the scar.

I was in the fourth grade. I was at a cousin's house. From his front porch, we raced around the house in opposite directions to see who returned to the porch first. Rounding a corner of the house, we met. That is, our heads met. A resounding blow was delivered to my head close to my left eye.

Blood oozed down my face. A large hematoma appeared. For days, I held my hand over my left eye, too embarrassed to let my classmates see the ugliness that my left eye presented.

Eventually the swelling receded, and following a few weeks of discoloration, healing was restored. However, a reminder had been left. When I look in the mirror, I see a small jagged scar, and I can still feel how fast my feet were flying around that house. I can still see the flashes of light as our heads collided.

You see, the story is in the scar.

Beneath my right foot and close to my big toe is a scar about one inch long.

I was just a lad, not even in school yet. Mom had a treadle Singer sewing machine. It was powered by a foot pedal. The user pushed back and forth on the foot pedal, turning a pully with a belt attached to it. Eventually all this motion and commotion sent energy upwards to the top of the sewing machine causing a needle and thread to do its mission.

That's more information than the reader really needs. However, some of my readers will exclaim, "We had one like that!" For most of you, the reaction is probably, "How odd!"

I spent most of my formative years from age one to five barefooted. That day, I was furiously pressing that foot pedal with my bare feet, and something went awry. My right foot ended up as an uninvited guest entangled between the pully and belt. The pully and belt won that day. Sadly, my right foot suffered a nasty gash.

To the best of my recollection, that was the first scar on my body. I admittedly don't see the underside of my right foot that often, but when I do, I'm reminded of that day when I tangled with a Singer treadle sewing machine and lost.

You see, the story is in the scar.

Most people in the course of life and living will collect scars. But why? God could easily have created our bodies to completely heal from cuts and wounds and leave no reminding scars.

Scars represent pain. A scratch, a cut, a surgical scar, a deep wound. There are so many causes for scars, and each one has a story that resides in that scar. Perhaps God wants us to contemplate our scars.

The really painful wounds are the ones you can't see. They cause lasting pain. No scab forms over the gash and promises imminent healing. Often, the wound festers and debilitates. Many times, those interior lacerations and mutilations will require some very powerful words to assist in healing.

And even when we find healing of these wounds through a miracle journey, there is still a scar.

Someone has left emotional scars on you. Or perhaps you were the one who left a scar on another. In the course of a lifetime, I can imagine we all will collect a few and will cause a few. We lose a spouse. We hear—or say—the words, "I don't love you anymore." We break trust or betray a friend. We hear cruel words as children. We are angry and say words that are never forgotten.

I had devastating wounds inflicted on my heart by someone I cared for deeply. Love and joy were ripped from me. Perhaps your life has been broken open by such a loss. The death of a cherished dream has left you feeling purposeless. Or someone has inflicted horrible abuse on your mind and soul. Or a disease is stripping you or your loved one of mental or physical capabilities. You've been the victim of a violent crime. Or ugly words screamed daily in your house have left you feeling beaten, alone, worthless, and hopeless.

Then there are the wounds of loss we all share—the loss of life as we knew it before 2020 brought COVID into our lives. We have all experienced loss as the pandemic raged through our communities. Some have lost jobs or homes or loved ones. Some have lost dreams that cannot be accomplished because of circumstances now. Some have lost relationships. Some families have been torn apart by opposing ideas. None of us are the same person we were twelve months ago.

You see, our stories are in our scars.

Someday my time here will be finished. I will approach the glow emanating from that City of Light.

As Jesus approaches me, I'll have my arms outstretched. I'll grasp His hands in mine. I know the story. I've known it all my life.

"I want to see Your scars!"

I'll gaze deeply at those scarred hands and see the story. The story of redemption. The story of forgiveness. I'm sure I'll cry as I read the story in His scars.

Even now, as I gaze into the scars on the hands of Jesus, an amazing metamorphosis is taking place. My scars are vanishing. They are being absorbed into the scars of Jesus.

I am being made perfect. Imagine that! Me, perfect! And it will only take a lifetime.

You see, dear friends, our entire story is in His scars.

But He was pierced for our transgressions,
He was crushed for our iniquities;
the punishment that brought us peace was on Him,
and by His wounds we are healed.
Isaiah 53:5

48

Heavenly Garment Shopping

Return to your fortress, you prisoners of hope;
even now I announce that I will restore twice as much to you.
Zechariah 9:12

This journey towards restoration has been long and arduous. As I write this, I've been traveling for a year and a half. Almost two years of sadness and pain. How long has it been for you?

Our journey has been filled with many setbacks. Burdened with feelings of rejection, abandonment, unworthiness. Tried by storms and fire. We've traveled through dry barren deserts of doubt. The signposts have sometimes been blurry. So often, we just wanted to give up.

Then someone would come along beside us and prophesy life into our dry bones. Glimmers of hope appeared, the possibility of dreams living again.

We have at last reached the outskirts of the land of restoration. The miracle of the journey is about to happen. No—now we see that the miracle has been happening all along!

I see the Jordan River just ahead. I'm done with traveling in circles in the wilderness. I want to cross into the Land of Promise. I'm so ready.

However, our garments are filthy. We've been through so much. What will the inhabitants of the City of Hope think of us, this ragtag bunch of wounded souls?

We need a change of clothing.

A figure approaches. I see it is Zechariah. God used him to prophesy to the exiles heading back home to Jerusalem, their city of hope. He's spoken to me, too, on this journey. We've become friends.

"I hear you need new clothes. I'll assist you there," he says.

But first, Zechariah tells me of a vision.

"One day, God showed me a vision. I saw Joshua standing before God. Satan was there, too, and as is his wont, he was accusing Joshua of all manners of evil. God rebuked him.

"The story is in my namesake book in the Old Testament. You can read it in chapter 3. I'll tell you the story now, Paul, but I'll insert your name instead of Joshua's because anyone on this miracle journey can hear and claim these words." (So that means, dear reader and fellow traveler, that you can replace my name with your own.)

"Then I was shown you, Paul, standing before the angel of the Lord. Satan was standing on the right side of the angel and began accusing you of all manners of lies and slander. 'He was just as wrong as she was; he deserved the deception; he deserved trust being broken; he did—'

"'Stop right there, Satan!' With that exclamation, God rebuked the devil. 'I chose this man. He's a burning stick snatched from the fire.'

"You were indeed a burning stick snatched from the fire, Paul. The smoke of deception clouded your thinking. The ashes of broken trust descended over you. There you stood, weary from the journey, with filthy clothes covered in soot.

"There were others there. The angel ordered them to remove your filthy clothes. The command came: 'Put rich garments on Paul.'

"So with that, let's go shopping in the Mall of Heavenly Garments."

I eagerly go with him. I am so ready.

Our first shop is located in Isaiah 52:1. "Clothe yourself with strength! Put on garments of splendor!" I do need restoration of strength after this journey. And garments of splendor would feel so good.

Next stop is Psalms 45:3. "Put on your sword, mighty warrior, clothe yourself with splendor and majesty." Another shop promising garments of splendor, but this one offers the accessories of a sword and majesty.

I am feeling mighty dapper. Where to next?

"Let's head in here," says Zechariah. It's Colossians 3:12.

Wow! This is for God's chosen people. Holy and dearly loved. *Loved!* What a heartening and healing word. I thought I'd lost love, but here's a shop saying I am dearly loved.

"As God's dearly loved son," Zechariah says to me, "these garments are most appropriate for you. Dress yourself in compassion and kindness. You have been hurt deeply. Along the miracle journey, many folks had compassion on you. It's time to show compassion to others."

I am decked out now. Yes, clothes appropriate for a son of the King. There's more here, but Zechariah is drawing me to another place.

What am I feeling? Is that pride? Are my new threads causing a bit of chest-puffing? Wasn't pride partly the cause of my downfall in love? I thought I had it made. A beautiful lady I trusted. A lady I loved deeply. A love sent from God. A love that came with a mission, a godly mission. We both knew it. Yes, I thought I had it all. But pride tripped me up. Pride carried a steep price tag. Abandonment, rejection, broken trust. The payment plan required this journey I've been slogging through.

Zechariah seems to know what I'm thinking. "You needed to be put under extreme pressure. You did have some bad characteristics that needed to be refined in fire."

As he speaks, we step into a low-key, nondescript store almost hidden among the others.

"Where are we? These clothes don't seem to match my regal splendor."

"This store has a vital article of clothing. It's the reason God sent you on this journey. There was something very important missing from your wardrobe."

I see that we are in 1 Peter 5. The store's mission statement is posted on the wall: GOD OPPOSES THE PROUD BUT GIVES GRACE TO THE HUMBLE.

"Clothe yourself in humility, child of God."

I am clothed with humility and find it comes with a free gift—grace!

"We are finished shopping now, aren't we?"

"On no, we have one more stop," says Zechariah. "The most important article of clothing is yet to come."

We enter Romans 13:14: *Clothe yourself with the Lord Jesus Christ.*

I break down in tears and sobs tear at my chest. The purpose of this entire shopping trip has come into focus.

There He stands, waiting for me.

I recognize the scars.

He recognizes mine.

He wraps His arms around me and holds me close. "I've been expecting you."

Clothe yourself with the Lord Jesus Christ.

I do.

"I want to stay here forever. Can I?"

"Later, just not now. You have a mission. There are so many hurting people out there. My sisters and brothers need someone to show them the way to Me. Others helped take off your filthy clothes. Now you are charged with doing the same. Put down road signs that will lead to Me. Now go."

As I turn to leave, Zechariah is gone. I see him off in the distance.

"Zach! Zach! Come back."

"No, Paul, there are so many others following you that also need new clothes. Go with your new clothing. Enter into the City of Hope, the city of restoration. And when you get there, I have a promise for you."

"What's the promise?"

I can't make out all he says as his voice fades away. I do hear him say "Chapter 9, verse 12."

The Message and the Messengers

In the beginning was the message, and the message was with God and the message was Love.

I can only imagine the sadness with which God looked down on Abraham as he was about to sacrifice Isaac. God stopped Abraham just in time to save his son. But as God saw Isaac about to be sacrificed, He had a glimpse of what He would need to do with His own Son—and that sacrifice would not be stopped.

His Son would be the message and the messenger.

However, as often happens, those to whom the message was sent killed the messenger.

Too late, though! The truth was out: There is hope! Redemption is available!

Now many other messengers are needed and called upon.

Imagine with me that there's a place in Heaven where messages are matched up with potential messengers. A prayer is prayed, a request is heard at the throne. It goes to Message Central.

Who will go with the message? Who is willing? Discussion ensues, and a messenger is chosen and dispatched with Heaven's answering word.

I was at peace that cold winter evening when one message arrived at my house. An email came: *My husband passed away recently. He died before he could accomplish his wish to pen a book about not waiting too long in life to do what's important. Retire early if possible. Volunteer. Travel. Have time with family. Honor God.*

That message had been handed to the deceased's grieving widow. She was now responsible for the message and had become a messenger herself. Her email explained that her husband had died within two weeks of the diagnosis. He had wanted to retire and write that book. Perhaps she could attempt to write it, but how to even start? Could I help?

In my imagination, I can see the meeting that might have taken place in Message Central Heaven as it was determined who would deliver the *Don't wait too long* message in book form. Guardian angels from all quarters of the writing world were summoned. They each gave testimony as to why their person would be qualified as messenger.

The book had great potential to change many lives. It held a message that could bring many folks back to a relationship with Jesus.

"We need an intellectual, a highly skilled writer for this task."

"It certainly needs to be someone with a seminary degree."

I assume the devil was there, too. He keeps tabs on his enemy, and his kingdom detected a threat.

One by one, each angel made their case for their own writer.

My angel presented his argument. "My guy wrote the book that inspired the deceased. We can easily arrange for him to write this one also."

"He has no qualifications!" came an emphatic objection.

"He's stubborn. He's tenacious," replied my advocate.

"Does he have any idea how difficult this task will be?"

"If he starts it, he will finish it," declared my angel.

And so, I was chosen to deliver the message of *Don't Wait Too Long.*

The devil, though, left that meeting with a smirk. "I'll defeat him."

Had I known the difficulty, the pain, the loneliness, the abandonment, the despair of broken trust that would follow, I would never have replied to that email.

But I did, and that's why you and I are here.

We talked, we met, and I fell in love with the messenger.

Then the message was lost in love. The devil had won before I even put fingertips on the keyboard.

But I had once again discovered love. A godly love, I believed. However, she was a messenger and did what messengers do. She left. The messenger was out of my life.

I was devastated. Abandoned and broken, but still holding this message. Adrift in high seas of pain, I wrote *Don't Wait Too Long*.

However, as that book ended, I realized it was just half done. The dead bones of my trust, hope, and joy lay scattered in a deep valley.

The message of *Don't wait too long!* finally hit home, right where I was living. I had not completed the task assigned me. A miracle journey was still required, the journey of restoration.

When I finally grasped the true meaning of the words, I set out on my own journey to restoration. What you just read is my journey. It's also the journey so many of you must take.

I have grappled with forgiveness for more than a year. How does one forgive the destruction of their spirit? The answer came in a powerful way yesterday as I sat down to write this chapter.

A reader of *DWTL* sent me a rendition of that favorite song I mentioned earlier, "The Love of God." This lady was in an abusive relationship and had been in and out of women's shelters for years. How do you possibly forgive someone who has done that to your life? When she discovered "The Love of God" was my favorite song, she sent one recording of it to me—just as I was preparing to write today.

As I've said, the third verse of that song is my favorite. It's the best description of God's love I have ever heard. I weep when I hear it. Today, it brought me into an emotional encounter with God.

> Could we with ink the ocean fill,
> And were the skies of parchment made,
> Were every stalk on earth a quill,
> And every man a scribe by trade…

That's not the end of the verse, but it was right then that the clouds parted.

"A scribe by trade!" That was me! And God had just shown me: The message I am always to write is about love. The love of God.

The message! Oh, the message. It's been there all along, from the very first promise given to a guilty pair—a promise that a Messenger would come with good news; to the night the Messenger was born into the world to save us; to my miracle journey when messengers helped me along the way; and on into forever. The message has always been there and will always be there. It is all about knowing the love of God.

Don't wait too long to discover the love of God. It's the only love that lasts.

As I listened to the song and the Spirit, God covered me in His love. It was a most incredible feeling of pure love washing over me. I fell to my knees and wept.

I have been tasked to write about God's love.

> The love of God is greater far
> Than tongue or pen can ever tell.
> It goes beyond the highest star
> And reaches to the lowest hell.
> The guilty pair, bowed down with care,
> God gave His Son to win;

> His erring child He reconciled
> And pardoned from his sin.

Imagine Adam and Eve, banned from their home in perfect Eden because of their sin. Have you felt the sadness of your sin?

Imagine the sadness God must have felt because of their disobedience—and the disobedience of His erring children. That included me! And you!

God is a God of passion. A holy passion. He loves us passionately. He showed His love for us this way: even while we were still sinners, Christ died to save us. (Romans 5:8 AP)

Then this holy, loving, redeeming God declared us His sons and daughters. He says we are joint heirs with His Son Jesus. Can you even grasp that? Everything God has promised Jesus also belongs to us. And just what is promised to Jesus? In a word, the universe! Yes, after everything evil and bad has been destroyed, what will remain will be perfect, and it is ours. We're heirs to a fortune.

Yes, thank you, God, I accept.

> O love of God, how rich and pure!
> How measureless and strong!
> It shall forevermore endure—
> The saints' and angels' song.

Earthly and human love can fail you, but His love endures forever (Psalm 136 verse 26 AP).

I recently received an email from a broken man who told me his wife of 23 years had divorced him. He had begged her to stay and prayed it would still work out, but the divorce was finalized the day before the email. Here are his exact words: "Pride got in the way. I have been angry, frustrated, confused, felt hopeless, numb, you name it." The email went on to explain how God had led him to a book I had written that spoke about the power of words. He admitted he should have said "I love you" and "I'm sorry" more often.

We have all had our mountains shaken! But God says to you and me, "Though the mountains be shaken and the hills be removed, yet my unfailing love for you will not be shaken" (Isaiah 54:10).

Here's what Paul wrote to the church at Rome and how he described the love of God:

> For I am convinced that neither death nor life, neither angels nor demons, neither the present nor the future, nor any powers, neither height nor depth, nor anything else in all creation, will be able to separate us from the love of God that is in Christ Jesus our Lord. (Romans 8:38-39)

This love of God lasts for eternity, forever and ever. It's nothing like the earthly love many of us were promised, only to be hurt when it didn't last. I hope all of my readers are able to recall a time in life when they were passionately in love. Remember that feeling? I do. It's amazing, isn't it? However, earthly love can be fickle. Distractions and busyness intrude, crowding out our first love. We get in our own way, too. Selfishness and pride make an appearance, and suddenly, some other person seems like a better fit.

We so often take our loved ones for granted. I'm so guilty of that. In my recent relationship, I left a message for myself. Shortly after our meeting where we fell in love, I took a bar of soap and scrawled on my bedroom dresser mirror "Don't take Her for granted."

Sadly, I did. I've paid a steep price in pain for that error, but I've discovered a love that I know will last. God will never break your trust. He will never abandon or forsake you. He loves you with an everlasting, holy, pure, undefiled love that will never end.

> Could we with ink the ocean fill,
> And were the skies of parchment made,
> Were every stalk on earth a quill,
> And every man a scribe by trade;
> To write the love of God above
> Would drain the ocean dry;
> Nor could the scroll contain the whole
> Though stretched from sky to sky.
>   -- Frederick Lehman 1917 and Unknown

As God's children and sisters and brothers of Jesus Christ, we are now carrying the message of the Father's love. Throughout my own journey towards restoration and my efforts to deliver the message, I have had many messengers come along beside me and give me hope.

I wish to honor them and dedicate this book to them.

When I stumbled, they caught me. When I fell, they picked me up. When I couldn't pray, they prayed. When I was too exhausted to go one more step on this journey, they carried me. They unwrapped my graveclothes and prophesied life to my dead spirit.

I give my thanks for the love of family and shoulders to cry on: to Carolyn, Gladys, Pearl, Glenda, Jr., Paul, Mervin, Wayne, Tom, Melissa, Rodrick, Jill, Trevor, Kristin, Mallory, Brady, Isaac, Blake, Kaylin, Elise, Gavin.

Friends carried a broken man to Jesus. So many times, I felt so alone. Yet as I look back, I realize how blessed I was to have messengers from God come alongside me just when it was needed most. Thank you to Marvin, Rita, Ivan, Fran, Susie, Perry, Jeremiah.

Jane, Doris, Dee, Elaine, Ina, and Zechariah, when it seemed forgiveness was nearly impossible, your amazing stories of forgiveness humbled me.

Thank you, Ashley, Lauren, Marcia, Colby, William, Diane, Kathy, Paula, the patrolman in South Carolina, and others, for small gestures as simple as a liked Facebook post. Yes, a very small token; but when your spirit is lacking, it doesn't take very much to lift you.

And to all of you who have walked, limped, cried, and struggled along with me while on your own journey towards restoration, I dedicate this book.

50

The End is the Beginning

We have come through the wilderness of devastation with the help of Jeremiah and Ezekiel, Zechariah, David, Isaiah, and others. Most importantly, the Holy Spirit has been our Guide. We have our new clothes. We're at the borders of the land of hope and restoration. We're ready for this.

How do I know you are ready for this? I don't know the specifics of your situation, but I know that God is the Great Designer—of the house under renovation that is you, of the worm that is transforming into a butterfly, of your miracle journey. He does things in the right time. I trust His hand in our lives.

That devastation that happened in our past? It happened. We'll take that history across the river with us. Healing doesn't mean we'll never feel the pain again, but the ache of a healed wound will not debilitate us. Instead of looking back, giving vent to the anger and desire for revenge, and agonizing over the past, we are looking ahead. We might think about the past and feel sad, but our eyes will be focused on today, the future, and life in the land of restoration.

God has watched over every step of our journey through the wilderness. His promise is restoration. His promises are what have kept us putting one foot in front of the other, and they will be what keep us going. We are no longer prisoners of what has hurt us, we are prisoners of hope. The God of all hope is our stronghold.

Now what?

There's a life to be lived in the land of promise. We may think *Whew, we made it!* but don't forget there are still many opponents that we must overcome in the land ahead—including giants!

The account of the Israelites entering their Promised Land is found in Deuteronomy and Joshua. Again and again, the promise is given: "Be strong and courageous! Do not be afraid and do not panic... For the Lord your God will personally go ahead of you. He will neither fail you nor abandon you" (Deuteronomy 31:6).

That's a promise we can claim as our own, in each of our days. Yes, we'll meet opposition ahead. But our God who created us and watches over us tells us not to be afraid. He has paid a heavy price to bring us to His kingdom and make us His children, we are dear to Him, and He will never abandon us. He has defeated evil. He has defeated death. He has paid for our brokenness and endured everything that makes it possible for our healing.

He has called each of us by name. It's personal with Him! He knows you. Knows everything about you. Knows what's going on with you. Knows your struggles. Knows your dreams and longings. Knows your weakness. Knows the deep wounds on your soul. And He says, "You are mine. Do not be afraid. I'm with you."

We are His treasured sons and daughters.

The night before the Israelites crossed the Jordan River into Canaan, Joshua sent this order throughout the camp: "Consecrate yourselves, for tomorrow the LORD will do amazing things among you" (Joshua 3:5). What amazing things will He be doing tomorrow in your life? In my life?

A long time ago on this journey, I asked you if you could believe God's promises. You have come this far by depending on Him. You have come this far because of Him. His long arm has brought you this far. Nothing is impossible for Him.

Amazing things are ahead for lives committed to Him. We've been through so much, but He's been working, preparing us for whatever He has planned.

This is not the end, but the beginning. Another of Moses' instructions to the people is also instructive for us: "Stay on the path that the Lord your God has commanded you to follow" (Deuteronomy 5:33). (The book of Deuteronomy is rich in wisdom for living in the land of promise.) He has redeemed us for a purpose. Life in this land we've finally reached will be sustained by His power. Stay on His path. Keep your eyes on your Guide and your ears open for His voice. Keep on dining divinely.

There will be more signposts and more people to help us along the way.

We've got the message, both in us and in our hands to deliver to others.

Courage will still be required, but we need not fear any giants or panic at any circumstance. Nothing we meet will be stronger than the One who lives in us, the One who has told us to be not afraid because He has overcome the world.

Don't forget to put down signposts for others to follow.

Now go and take the land!

*And now these three remain: faith, hope, and love.
But the greatest of these is love.
1 Corinthians 13:13*

After Words

I'm aware most readers don't read the afterword to a book. Once they read "The End," they believe the author—that it is truly "the end."

I believe the few readers who go through the next pages with me will be folks who have been hurt or are still hurting. You are grasping for any small word of encouragement and hope to bring some semblance of closure to your grief.

Let me say that I know many of the "after words" in these next pages are repetitious. You have already read them, either in this volume or the previous *Don't Wait Too Long* or in another work of mine. But I'm compelled to write them one more time.

There are two reasons for this. First, healing is a process that does repeat. You who have gone through devastation and are now on the border of the land of restoration have experienced this. Sometimes it feels as if you are going in circles—you go over the same ground, again and again. Or you may even feel you've gone backward. Second, these are things I must write one more time for myself—and then I'm done with my lamentations!

During the summer and fall of 2020, I spent hours every day on my parents' old glider. With my Bible and various books about relationship breakups and forgiveness, I contemplated my horrible emotional pain. I journaled my thoughts about pain and loss on paper and kept notes on my phone. I marked many Bible verses that assisted in healing. I revisit these signposts often. You've read many of them here.

However, when the time came to write this follow-up to *Don't Wait Too Long*, I wasn't able to bring those words and thoughts out of my heart and mind and run them through my fingertips to the keyboard. *The Miracle Journey* was in my heart but refused to be channeled to my fingers.

I was emotionally unable to function as a writer—but my tongue still worked quite well. So once a week, I'd meet with my editor, Elaine Starner, and I'd speak straight from the pain flowing from my heart. She recorded and then transcribed and edited my conversation. This all took extra time and extra work. I was okay with that, since I was "writing" as the healing process was taking place.

My thanks go to her. During the past two years of grief, she has been patient as I paced, wept, and procrastinated. There were times she even encouraged me to remove sections from *The Miracle Journey* because she believed they sounded a bit harsh.

It's true we often react harshly to rejection. It's true that we hurt the people we love the most. I loved deeply and grieved deeply and at times allowed my pain to be expressed in ways I'm not proud of.

Recently, I've thought about the power of our words and the power of our tongue. The third chapter of James is entitled

"Taming the tongue." Verse 5: "The tongue is a small part of the body, but it makes great boasts." A small spark can set a great forest on fire. Verse 6: "The tongue is also a fire, a world of evil among the parts of the body."

The words we allow our tongues to speak can destroy people or heal people. "Reckless words pierce like a sword, but the tongue of the wise brings healing" (Proverbs 12:18).

Here's a tidbit of wisdom: Be wise! Let your words bring healing, not destruction.

So, to you remaining few readers, allow me to be very honest and vulnerable. Many in our band of broken people have found healing and have entered the land of restoration. But I'm sure there are a few hurting men still with us. To them I say, it's okay to cry about your pain. It's okay to talk to people about what you're going through. It's okay to be vulnerable. Don't allow yourself to shut down and become bitter. Society tells us many things that aren't true: "Be tough. Big boys don't cry." Rubbish! Big and small boys and men need to cry. "Sticks and stones may break my bones, but words will never harm me." That's the biggest lie ever told. Getting hit by a stick can inflict bodily pain that heals. Words can inflict damage that destroys lives. I'm sure many of you still hear painful words ringing in your mind years after they were thrown at you. By the end of our conversation, I'll show you how to begin proper healing from those words that have been so damaging.

What are those words that have hurt you so badly? Don't allow them to destroy you. Talk about them. Email them to me. I'll pray for your continued healing. (My email is on the "Get to Know Paul Stutzman" page at the back of the book.)

Two recent tragedies have made me ponder the power of words and conversations. A friend of mine lost her 22-year-old daughter in a tragic accident. This same lady's mother had just passed away two weeks before the accident. I wonder what the last conversation was like with my friend and her mother. I know how much they loved each other. I suspect it was, "Mom, I love you so much." I had heard her speak those words so often before. I also wonder about my friend's last conversation with her 22-year-old daughter. They were so close.

My last conversation with this beautiful and talented 22-year-old girl was at their kitchen counter, as I was getting beat by her at a game of cards. Her whole life was ahead of her. Seeing her grandmother in failing health had put a love and a desire to help hurting people in her heart. She was in grad school, pursuing a degree in health care. Why would God allow such a person's life to end so tragically in an instant?

Several weeks prior, I had been at calling hours for my last surviving uncle. He had passed away at age 100. Bookends of life. One lived 100 years; the other, 22.

In reality, whether the years are 22 or 100 matters little in the scope of eternity. We so often focus too much on "now." On what we call "time." Time really does not exist. Only clocks do. Clocks mark off increments of "now." Eternity is what we should spend more time contemplating.

It's what we send ahead that matters. That's what we will be judged on someday. Perhaps the 22-year-old had already sent enough ahead that it was time for her reward. Her earthly father and her heavenly Father awaited her in Heaven.

My uncle spent most of his 100 years anticipating his arrival in that celestial city, as he called it.

What are you sending ahead? Will there be people in Heaven because of your efforts?

The second tragedy involved two boys from the town where my son attended college. His friends knew these boys. One was 12; the other, 11. While snowmobiling, the 12-year-old hit a wire that lacerated his throat. The 11-year-old held his friend's hand as he bled to death. Could you even imagine the final conversation between those two boys? Imagine the shock and horror of the parents when the news reached them? What was their last conversation with their son? Surely, they had expected him to return home.

Someday you, too, will have a last conversation. It may be hearing someone else's last words, or it will be your last utterance.

Fifty-five years ago, I was with my friend when he had a bicycle accident that took his life. I was riding along beside him down a country road. One second he was beside me; then he was gone. The gravel on the road shoulder pulled him off to the side, and unfortunately it happened by a bridge, where his head hit the retaining wall. That was 55 years ago, and the last words of my friend still ring clearly in my mind. Only thirty minutes before, we were at the end of my cousin's driveway, deciding which direction to turn for a night bike ride. My friend said the fatal words that I can still hear. "Let's go left."

The power of words. The power of our choices.

Most words are just that, words spoken in our everyday lives. There are, however, times when words change the trajectory of our lives.

I remember some of those times.

"The surgery went well, but the cancer is malignant and has metastasized to the liver."

"How long do we have, Doctor?"

"Several months to several years."

Those words changed me profoundly. It's why I'm writing books instead of managing restaurants. I retired early and hiked the Appalachian Trail in search of healing after my wife's death. My first book, called *Hiking Through,* chronicles that journey. I thought I was writing to share the adventure, but it turns out that *Hiking Through* has helped thousands of hurting folks find healing.

That book is also the reason I found another love I had prayed for. God blessed me with an amazing lady. We both knew God had brought us together. However, He brought us together for a purpose—to write a book together that would help thousands of people not wait too long to make good choices.

I pursued the lady, but failed to pursue the task that God had for us. By not pursuing that task, I failed her during our courtship. I was blinded by love and completely failed to guard my heart. And because I failed her in that regard, I received some of the most hurtful, devastating words of my life. *He's better on paper. He's better for my lifestyle.* In one second, my life collapsed and a family I loved was lost to me.

As I'm writing this afterword, it's two years, to the day, that she met her new man.

Just the previous day, life was grand. I was at peace. I was in love. Her text message that day read, "I thank God for you in my life. God brought us together forever. I love you." Her forever lasted 24 hours.

I was devastated. Destroyed. For two years now, those words brought so much pain, so many sleepless nights, thousands of hours of endless thoughts and questions swirling through my mind.

How could she possibly end what God had brought together?

Following another sleepless night recently, I cried out to the Holy Spirit, "Why? I need an answer. How could she love me one day and change her mind the next day? Why do I suffer this debilitating pain and she gets to float away on a Magic Carpet ride? Why do I grieve so hard?"

When my wife passed away, I wanted to know why I felt the way I felt. I wanted to understand what grief really was. I purchased numerous books about folks who had lost a spouse. But the grief I was experiencing in these last years was so much harder to deal with than the loss of my wife. Why?

I heard the Holy Spirit's reply. *Your wife passed away through no choice of her own. She didn't break your trust. She passed away, and there was no longer any possibility of a further relationship with her. You understood that, and with time, reconciled yourself to that reality.*

The Holy Spirit continued. *I do understand what you're going through. It happened to me, too. Your pain is because of a betrayal. Your best friend, the person you loved and trusted, betrayed you. They often don't deliberately intend to betray you; they just don't realize the consequences of their actions. They do what seems best for them at the moment. Judas betrayed me. He did not understand the consequences of his actions.*

To my readers who think I'm comparing my pain to the betrayal of Jesus, I have good news for you. I am! That's the beauty of following and falling in love with Jesus. At that last supper, Jesus was a man. A human. He felt love and betrayal just like you have. He understands what you're feeling. And now He is the only one who will—for a 100 percent certainty—never leave you or fail you.

I told you earlier I'd tell you where healing starts. Here it is.

You received the devastating news: I'm leaving you. I've found someone better. Our marriage is over. I'm sorry, but your spouse has two weeks to live. There's been a tragic accident…

Psalms 69 might describe what you're feeling: "Save me, O God, for the waters have come up to my neck. I sink in the miry depth, where there is no foothold. I have come into the deep waters; the floods engulf me."

I'm sure many of you will relate to that lament from King David. Later in that same chapter in verse 29, he cries, "I am in pain and distress; may your salvation, O God, protect me."

And there is the answer.

When you've sunk low enough, you will find solid footing only in Jesus Christ, the Man who felt every emotion and pain you will ever feel. He now invites you to believe in Him, embrace Him, Love Him.

I believe God gave me that message to deliver to a lost world and a love to help me deliver it. Together, we were to write a book about not waiting too long. I failed!

I'm in pain because of my own failure. Why, God, did I fail you so badly? Why did I not cherish the gift you gave me? Why did she give me up so easily?

I heard the Holy Spirit's reply. *The devil broke up your relationship. It's what he does. He loves to destroy relationships. He realized you two were a threat to him if you determined to honor the reason God brought you together.*

But why do I suffer this loss so much and she doesn't?

Do you ever wish she would experience the same suffering you've gone through? If you could send this suffering back on her, would you?

That dialogue gave me brief pause before answering: Absolutely not.

To my hurting readers, when you can say that about the person who gave you devastating words and hurt you badly, and when you mean it, you are well on your way to healing.

I actually meant it.

(A part of me slyly desired the "check engine light" to come on in the magic carpet she seemed to be floating on. I just chuckled a bit and realized my humor was slowly returning.)

Previously, I mentioned a few books that were helpful to my understanding about my pain. I'll list a few.

First, the one I described as being touched by a feather. That title is *Getting Past Your Breakup* by Susan J. Elliott.

The other book, written by a man suffering in a situation eerily similar to mine, hit me with brutal truths. That title is *Learning How to Heal a Broken Heart.* It was written by Marvin Scholz.

Following my wife's death, I purchased numerous books on grief. There are many good ones, but I'll recommend one. It's entitled *A Grace Disguised.* Jerry Sitter, the author, lost his wife, mother, and daughter in a car accident. Imagine that. Three generations gone in an instant. If you're grieving the loss of a spouse or a family member and question the how, why, when, and even the if of recovery, this book will give you valuable insights as you trudge through your valley of pain.

During the past two years I was faced with a dilemma: To forgive or not to forgive. I believed in forgiveness because that was what I was taught all my life. However, up to this point in my life, I've never had to forgive such a devastating blow to my mind and spirit. How does a person forgive another who has inflicted such horrible pain?

Granted, forgiveness is surely easier if the offender realizes the pain they have inflicted, admits wrongdoing, and asks for forgiveness. But what if they don't? You must still forgive. But how?

I knew I needed to forgive for my own wellbeing and sanity, but I soon discovered forgiveness was not as simple as I thought it would be. I needed to discover why forgiveness was so difficult. I needed to understand the concept of forgiveness. More research followed. Again, I purchased books and discovered new insights on forgiveness.

My favorite forgiveness book was a small volume entitled *Forgiving What You'll Never Forget.* There are several books out there with the same title. This one is written by Dr. David Stoop.

(Several books with the same title, you ask? Yes, I'm deviating. Book titles can't be copyrighted. Contents of the book are under copyright, but not the title. You could write a book and call it *War and Peace* or *Profiles in Courage.* These are the kind of things one learns from reading the afterword.)

Back to the task at hand.

As I journaled and grieved and hurt and contemplated my pain during the 2020 glider summer, I also contemplated thoughts about forgiveness and relationship breakups by famous writers. Of course, I captured them in my phone, and they reside among dozens of Scripture verses that assisted in my healing. I'll quote a few for your reading pleasure.

The first one is from Ernest Hemingway: "The most painful thing is losing yourself in the process of loving someone too much, and forgetting that you are special too." Thanks, Ernie, but I don't feel very special.

Another from an anonymous author reads: "When you love someone more than they deserve, surely, they will hurt you more than you deserve." (I'm not sure if I actually agree with that, but since it's on my phone, I included it.) People do deserve to be loved deeply and completely. I did, and in my opinion, my friend deserved that kind of love. Because I loved that deeply is the reason I grieve so deeply. That's what lost love does. It hurts. It should hurt. If it didn't, it wouldn't have been love.

Here's another from my phone archives: "Never lie to someone who trusts you, and never trust someone who lies to you." I hate lies! I was taught to never lie. God hates lies. 1

Corinthians 13:6 declares, "Love does not delight in evil, but rejoices with the truth."

However, is withholding truth when truth needs to be spoken similar to lying? I have been guilty of withholding truth and perhaps have even been a bit deceptive at times. That is not a good characteristic. There is one benefit to being destroyed and broken. When you go to Jesus for rehab, you can be put back together and eliminate those bad characteristics. I did just that.

Following the breakup, I attempted to date. Sadly, I wasn't ready yet for another relationship. I needed more than 24 hours. My dates consisted of sitting there and crying about my loss. I don't recommend going that route. It's unlikely to succeed.

However, one lady gave me an amazing compliment. She didn't intend to be complimentary, though. "Paul, you're too honest," she said. Inwardly, I smiled. Honesty is just better. You never have to worry about getting tripped up in a falsehood.

I'll leave you with an amazing quote about forgiveness from the author Mark Twain. Yes, the creator of *Tom Sawyer* and *Huckleberry Finn*. "Forgiveness is the fragrance that the violet sheds on the heel that has crushed it."

Finally, to the handful of folks still with me, a brief update on coming attractions.

I'm currently journaling thoughts and ideas for a men's devotional book that all ladies should read. It will be a compilation of stories about life and death, love and pain. I suppose it's a book about life and living—a book I talked about writing even before *Hiking Through*. My journeys through the past years have changed the original concept, though. This book will be nothing like my younger self envisioned.

Through my pain, I now feel other folks' pain so deeply and desire to help hurting people. I invite you to assist me in doing that. If you want to share some of your own journey, email me. Perhaps you will also help others on the Miracle Journey.

I also have a children's book being released this summer. It's entitled *The Cloud Factory*. Yes, I have finally reached the pinnacle of my intellectual writing skills!

Thank you once again to my readers. This has been a different journey than most of my physical journeys. In reality, this has been the most difficult journey of my life. However, I cling to numerous lifelines in the Scriptures, especially the one from Psalms 34:18: "The Lord is close to the brokenhearted and saves those who are crushed in spirit."

Peace and healing in your life.

Paul Stutzman

GET TO KNOW PAUL STUTZMAN at
www.paulstutzman.com
www.facebook.com/pvstutzman
pstutzman@roadrunner.com

OTHER BOOKS BY PAUL STUTZMAN
The Wandering Home Series (Fiction)
Book One: The Wanderers
Book Two: Wandering Home
Book Three: Wander No More

Adventure Memoir
Hiking Through
  One Man's Journey to Peace and Freedom on the Appalachian Trail
Biking Across America
  My Coast-to-Coast Adventure and the People I Met Along the Way
Mississippi Misadventure
  (Formerly a section of *Stuck in the Weeds*)
Pilgrims: *On the Camino de Santiago*
  (Formerly a section of *Stuck in the Weeds*)
The 13th Disciple
  (Also available in stores, under the title *Hiking Israel*)

Spiritual Memoir
Don't Wait Too Long

With Author Serena Miller
More Than Happy: The Wisdom of Amish Parenting

"Young fella, where you frum? Why you running away?"

Leroy L. Jackson, Jr. detected it immediately. Others could see it, too, even if Johnny Miller wouldn't admit it. He was running. Whether he was running from home or toward home, he did not know.

Johnny Miller was twenty-three when he died the first time. The truck hit him as he pedaled along a Texas road, biking across the country in an attempt to find, somehow, somewhere, a new life.

His old life had vanished like a vapor. He thought he had lost everything on the day he lost his dear Annie. But he will lose far more before finally finding the way that leads to home... and life and peace.

Johnny Miller is back home again, farming the land he loves in a quiet Amish community in Ohio. But although he's not physically wandering, he is still wondering. Wondering why he is restless. Wondering why he feels that some piece of his life is not yet in place. Wondering why, when he was medically "dead," he was met by his wife, who told him his time to enter Heaven had not yet come—he was still needed on earth.

After Paul Stutzman lost his wife to breast cancer, he sensed a tug on his heart—the call to pursue a dream. Paul left his stable career, traveled to Georgia, and took his first steps on the Appalachian Trail. What he learned during the next four and a half months on the trail changed his life—and will change readers' lives as well.

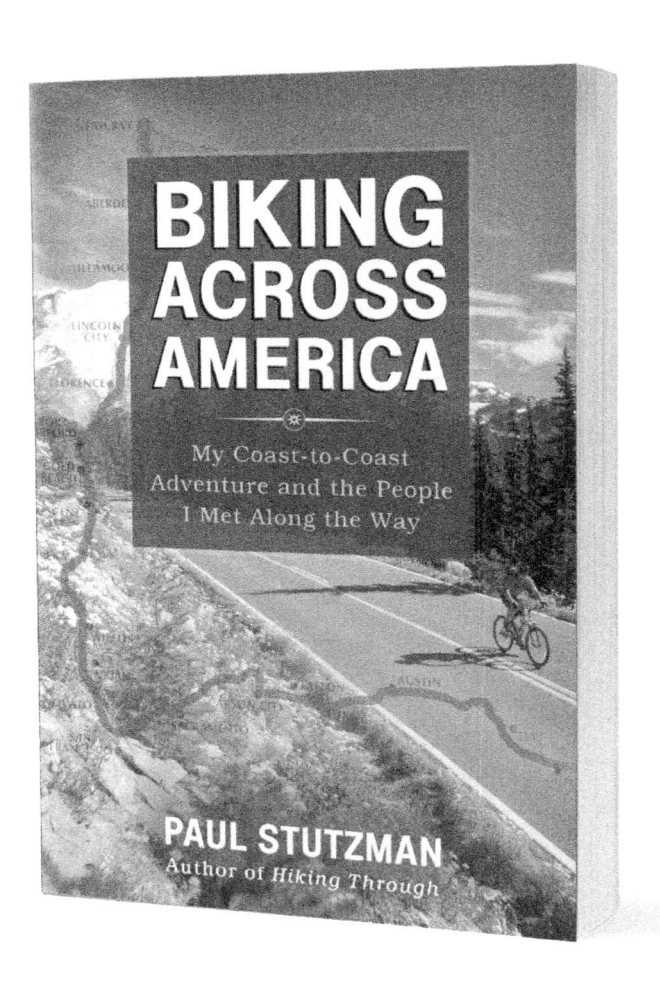

Paul Stutzman trades his hiking boots for a bicycle and sets off from Neah Bay, Washington, ending in Key West, Florida, traversing 5,000 miles. Along the way, he encounters nearly every kind of terrain and weather the country has to offer—as well as fascinating people whose stories readers will love.

MISSISSIPPI Misadventure

PAUL STUTZMAN
author of *Hiking Through*

"Imprisoned in my kayak, I leaned back and wondered if this choice I had made was perhaps the most foolish, ill-advised choice of my entire life." Attempting to kayak the length of the Mississippi River, Paul rethinks his choices and his spiritual journey. (Previously published as a segment of *Stuck in the Weeds)*

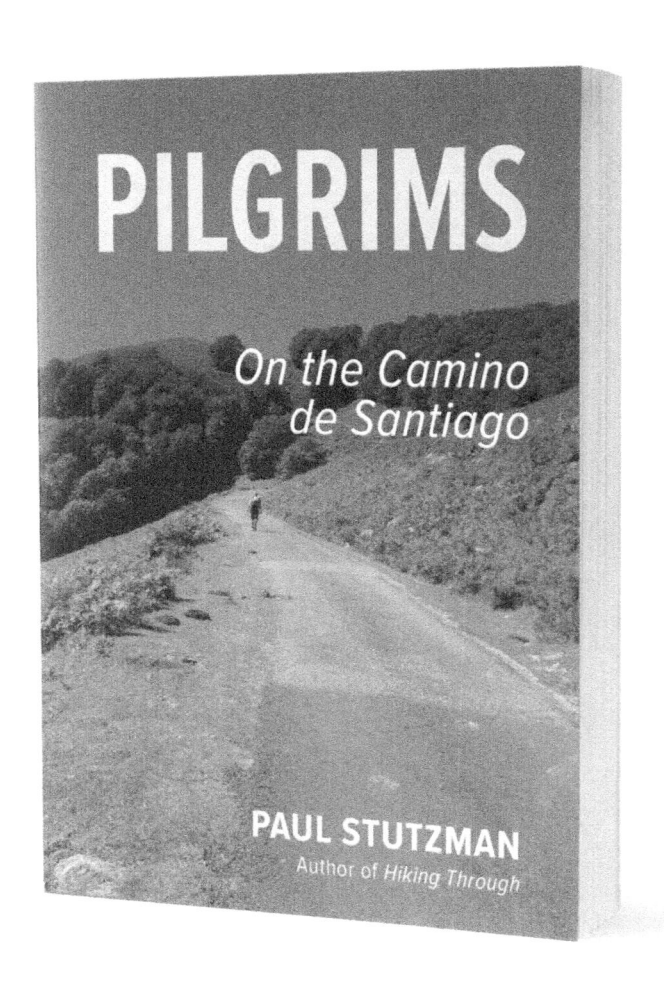

PILGRIMS

On the Camino de Santiago

PAUL STUTZMAN
Author of *Hiking Through*

In a pilgrimage to find answers and clarity on personal and faith issues, Paul Stutzman hikes a famous trail in Spain and ponders how choosing to be a disciple of Christ affects the pilgrimage of every believer. (Also published as a segment of *Stuck in the Weeds*)

On a hike through Israel, Paul Stutzman and his friend Craig visit places that were prominent in the life and ministry of Jesus. Paul is seeking two things: to better know the human Jesus and to find the answer to a question that has puzzled him for years: What does it mean to follow Jesus? (Also found under the title *Hiking Israel*)

DON'T WAIT TOO LONG

PAUL STUTZMAN

In a deeply personal reflection, Paul writes about two love stories during two years of his life. Don't postpone dreams. Don't wait until the perfect "someday." Paul's message is urgent and applicable to your walk of faith and your human relationships.

Author Serena B. Miller talks with Amish parents to discover principles of parenting and family life in Amish homes. Paul Stutzman contributes from his own Amish and Conservative Mennonite upbringing.

With practical takeaways for every family—regardless of religion—on how to raise happy, responsible, productive kids.

Made in the USA
Monee, IL
21 September 2021